HIDE OR SEEK

The Journeys of My Inner Child

CHARLES C. WOODS

WESTBOW
PRESS®
A DIVISION OF THOMAS NELSON
& ZONDERVAN

WestBow Press books may be ordered through booksellers or by contacting:

WestBow Press
A Division of Thomas Nelson & Zondervan
1663 Liberty Drive
Bloomington, IN 47403
www.westbowpress.com
844-714-3454

Bible scripture quoted from the King James Version of the Bible.

ISBN: 978-1-6642-1060-8 (sc)
ISBN: 978-1-6642-1061-5 (hc)
ISBN: 978-1-6642-1059-2 (e)

Library of Congress Control Number: 2020921363

Print information available on the last page.

WestBow Press rev. date: 11/10/2020

PREFACE

LET ME INTRODUCE myself. I am Charles Woods, known to my family and childhood friends as Bubby. I was raised in Tuckerman, a small town in Arkansas. I lived there until 1977, and then I moved away to finish college in Missouri. I graduated from Tuckerman High School in 1973. Six months later, I attended Southern Baptist College (Williams Baptist College) in Walnut Ridge, Arkansas. I received my associate of arts there. I married Christine, my wife, during that time.

After graduating from college, we moved to Bolivar, Missouri, to attend Southwest Baptist College (Southwest Baptist University), and I received my bachelor of arts in 1979. When I graduated from Southwest Baptist, Christine and I went to do missions in North Dakota for two years. We moved from North Dakota to Oklahoma to pastor Graham Baptist Church for four years. We moved again, this time to Kansas City, Missouri, to attend Midwestern Baptist Theological Seminary. In 1989, I graduated with my master of divinity degree.

We lived in Missouri for the next twenty years, pastoring at Trimble Baptist Church and Lawson Baptist Church. Then we went back into mission work, as the director of missions of Twin Rivers Baptist Association. While ministering there, I earned my master practitioner degree in neurolinguistic programming from LeadPlus, located in Woodstock, Georgia. We moved to California in 2006 to pastor at Linden Baptist Church and then to Marysville to pastor Feather River Baptist Church. While pastoring here, I am also the director of mission for the Sierra Butte Baptist Association.

We have two children and six grandchildren. With our children's loving mates, it makes an even dozen of us all. We love them and will always share how much we love them with anyone.

For many years, I thought about writing some of the stories from my life, but I did not feel the freedom to do so. Anytime a person opens their life, they take a chance of losing a part of themselves. I write this to gain a part of me that has been missing. We cannot help what people think. Everyone views life from their history—and not just history that happened yesterday, but from the time they were born. Someone told me once that our childhood life has nothing to do with who we are today. I do not agree with that statement.

How many dreams do you have about who you are? How many times have things happened that seem to make no sense? Everything that has been and will be is connected. Working to make things better is important to others as well as yourself. The history of the little me has not been shared before this short book. The years that this book covers are from birth through eight years old. There may be times when I take a moment to talk about my life when I am older, but it is only for a clarification of my life in the past.

I am not sharing this to say I know all there is to know. I have lots more to learn, and I am giving myself more years to do this. Sometimes people want answers right now and are unwilling to let things play out over time. This little boy, Bubby, so named by his older brothers, lived in fear until recently. I think everybody has a young them still alive inside. It is not a double personality; it is the same person. We cannot always hide who we are. Our lifelong beliefs come out in some way at given times. If you are unable to understand something I have said, do not worry. Whatever it is, if you do not understand, it will become clear at another time.

As you read about the little guy in this book, take heart that he is doing great. He sees himself as a normal person. He is who he was meant to be. He is willing to give up everything for everyone so that they will be happier and healthier in their lives. The kindest people are those who seek the best for others. People may be afraid to be who they are for various reasons. Do not be afraid of yourself. You would not be here if there were not a reason. The things in your life shape you and make you who you are. Your life is important to others. If you have not discovered this yet, it is time.

It is not strange voices that some people hear sometimes. They are a reality of who you are and the you that is there. Bubby went through a lot in his little life, and he saw things that maybe he should not have seen. He did not look away or run from the pain. He stayed who he is, and he is not ashamed of himself. Sometimes it seemed like he would have a short life. I thought the same thing at one time. In these chapters, take an adventure with him and then go back and claim or reclaim yourself.

ACKNOWLEDGMENTS

AT THIS MOMENT, I wish to say thank you to the people who have helped me come to this place to share the life and times of Bubby. The first and foremost person is my wife, Christine. We have been together since 1972. We became soulmates and believers in Jesus in the first three years we were together. She has supported me all these years. She was my first real date, and I was hers. She moved next door to me in 1972, and we soon became each other's life. Jesus made the bond even more reliable. Whenever I did a paper for school, she was there to make it look better. Even today, that has not changed. I am not ashamed to also tell you that we committed to a pure life when we first met and agreed to save that part of us until we were married. We kept our agreement with each other, and there was never anybody else in our lives. Christine and I raised two beautiful children. They, their mates, and their kids mean the world to us. We have had disagreements as all do, but we were always ready to work out anything that came up.

She has done so many things in this life to impress me and make me so happy to be her husband. We know each other very well, but we know we have not seen all there is to see in each other. As she proofreads this book, the thought was evident that there was more to learn. There have been times when I was ridiculously hard to understand. Bubby was unknown—even to her—but she had the first opportunity to see him for who he was and is. As we approach our forty-seventh anniversary, I hope the next forty-seven years will be even more significant. I will, at some time, write many pages about this wonderful woman who chose me, so many years ago, to spend her life with.

Thank you, Christine, for being there all these years and the ones to come. You make me healthy and ready to face new challenges all the time.

The next person I want to thank is Becky Grimes. Christine and I met her around 2001. Becky was working hard in camps for girls, boys, and teenagers. She became a trusted friend who has proven that you can find people like her in this life. Becky would do anything we ask, so I am careful what I ask. When looking for someone to help proofread this book, she was the first person Christine and I thought of. She agreed to do so, and here it is for you to read. Her help through the years, with the help of Wade, her husband, is so appreciated. Her love for teaching and learning makes her a strong lady. Her real strength, though, comes from her relationship with Jesus. Her witness—and Wade's witness—has been invaluable through the years for so many people, especially young people. Thanks again for taking on the task of helping me complete this book.

The next person to help me by proofing the work I have done is Mildred (Millie) Berryhill. We met Millie when she began to come to church, and she has been a great help. She is a lady who has done many incredible things in her life. Her life story could fill a book. She loves to read and quilt. She is a friend to Christine and me. We have taken short trips with her, and each trip is filled with her telling us about the beautiful things she has accomplished during her life. Thank you, Millie, for taking the time to help me with my mistakes during this writing. With people like these, I find peace and comfort.

The next person to thank is Laurie McShea, my office assistant for more than twelve years. She has always been there to cheer me on in doing my writings. She has read them and encouraged me to continue them. Everyone needs people to encourage them. In my dry days, she would ask me how the book was coming and tell me that I should get back to writing it. She was always asking me about another book I am writing while doing this one as well. *The Land of Nis* is its title. I have finished it and waiting to publish it. She recently moved and is no longer my assistant. I will miss her being there to cheer me on. Like you will see, when you read *Hide or Seek*, she is one of those friends who had to move away. Christine and I wish her and her husband, Shaun, all the blessings possible.

Someone did not know they helped me believe it was time to write this book. During the Campfire event in California in 2018, I was privileged to work with Mike Bivins and Disaster Relief. We spent many hours and days doing what we could to help the people affected by the fires. Our friendship grew, and he has become a person of influence for me. He invited me to share a short message at the yearly banquet for Disaster Relief. I was ready to share what God had given me to share. I felt I was meant to share more that night. That meeting was the first time I had ever opened myself up to share the little me who also went through a fire and lost loved ones. Mike received the message with tearful, heartfelt affection. That encouragement has brought me to the place where I am ready to allow the little boy to share his life with others. Thanks, Mike, and blessings to you.

A group has supported me each time I told stories from my past. This group has heard more than any other. Some of the stories were repeated over and over, and they did not flinch at any time. Their support to allow me to be me has also encouraged me to begin this part of my journey. Feather River Baptist Church is a special and unique church of friends and people. The foundation I have in Christ has been shaped through all the churches and people I have worked with. I realize what God can do through people of faith. Blessings on each of you—and thank you!

TABLE OF CONTENTS

INTRODUCTION

Search me, O God, and know my heart: try me, and know
my thoughts: And see if there be any wicked way in me,
and lead me in the way everlasting.

—Proverbs 139:23–24 (KJV)

I HEAR CRYING where there was once laughing. Why do I hear crying?
I hear it from deep within the recesses of my heart. There it is again; do
you hear it also? Can you help me? Do you know why I hear crying?

How many people hear crying every day but do nothing about it?
Where is the crying coming from? Think for a moment and listen to the
voice you hear. Does it sound like someone you know or knew?

Stop hiding and start seeking who it is that cries out to be heard. Not
everyone will have things in their lives that need such attention. If there
is any thought or voice you hear, then seek what can be a life-changing
moment—not for the grownup you have become but for the child hidden
inside, waiting to be heard and waiting to find the person they want to
trust. Trust is gained slowly and needs to be nurtured to be healthy.

CHAPTER 1
PAINFUL YET NEEDED

HOW MUCH PAIN can a person endure in life before they come to a breaking point? To the point of stopping or finding that you move forward into the life set before you. Let me start with the day Dad let me drive down the muddy road. This event happened less than a month before the fire. My dad, one of my three older brothers (the youngest of the three), and I were coming home. We had gone into town to pick up a few needed things for home and for Mom. We had to drive seven miles on the highway. I said highway because everything else was either dirt, mud, or gravel roads. Once we reached our turnoff, we would be on a mud road. It was wintertime, and there had been lots of rain that year. The road to the house from the highway was about half a mile. It was straight and only one lane. If someone were coming from the other direction, we would have to wait for them to come to the end of the road.

The road was muddy, but that was not all. Grooves had been cut into the road from so many cars traveling on it. These grooves, ruts as we called them, were deep. The cars would drag the bottom from the highway to the house. Everyone knew to drive their car inside these ruts and not go out of them. The day before I got to drive, my brother drove down the road. He got out of the ruts, and Dad told him to get back in them. He listened to Dad and let the car drop back into the ruts. At this point, the car would steer itself, and there was no need to keep your hands on the steering wheel. It was like one of those theme park rides once you started

1

down the road. You were not to stop or let off the gas pedal. If you did, you would get stuck. When you got stuck, you either got out and pushed or walked to get someone with a tractor to pull you out. My brother made it all the way home.

Since I was only five years old, Dad let me sit in his lap to steer the car. I could not reach the foot pedals, and Dad would do that part. I had done it many a time before on good roads. There was never a problem with me keeping it on the road, but I did not realize Dad had his hand close on the bottom of the steering wheel in case something went wrong. This time, he did not have his hands to help guide. He thought the ruts would do all that for him. He pointed the car down the road and said, "It's all yours, Bubby."

I was ready. My hands gripped the wheel tight—as if our lives depended on it. There were ditches on both sides of the car, and they were full of water. On my own, I jerked the wheel and had the car out of the ruts and on higher ground. The bottom was not dragging across the ground as before. I saw my brother looking at Dad and waiting to hear Dad tell me to get back in the ruts as he did with him the day before.

He was right. Dad did not wait to tell me to get back into the ruts or grab the wheel to do so. I continued to keep the car on the high part of the road and was doing fine. Dad, once again, told me to get back into the ruts. My brother was watching and waiting to see Dad take the wheel. I am sure he was smiling because Bubby was not doing what Dad had told him to do. Just before Dad could say it all to me again, I spoke up.

Speaking up was something I never did because everyone was always talking for me. When I spoke in my defense of getting out of the ruts, I explained to Dad that the old ruts were worn out, and we needed to make new ones to drive on.

Dad did not say a word, and he let me stay on the high ground.

My brother said, "I wish I had said that yesterday."

Dad laughed, and they looked at each other and then back at me. I just kept driving like nothing had been said or done. I still remember that moment and think about it many times, especially when I feel like I am in a rut of my own. That is when we need to take the high ground and make new paths in our lives.

Then there was the trip to pick fruit in Michigan at harvest time. I walked in every step that Dad did—never leaving his side. I looked up at this giant of a man with such tenderness. It lifted a small boy's hopes and spirit to heights that would give me a life full of strength. The family would work among the fruit trees and blueberry bushes like we were one.

In Michigan, to make better money for when we went back home, we lived in a row of houses meant for harvest workers. One day, we were all in the apple orchard. All the workers spent the whole day picking apples. I remember the apples being green. The owner's son and I played together while everyone else worked. Everyone gathered for their pay at the end of the day.

Some days, they would get into a rotten apple-throwing contest. Not at targets—but at each other. It was time to hide because they did not care who they hit. The purpose was just to hit somebody. My brothers and Dad were always up for a game of apple throwing. They were good at it—as they were at almost everything.

I wanted to be beside Dad every minute of the day, and that day was no exception. I watched everyone getting hit over and over. Some apples were so rotten that they would burst into mush as soon as someone was hit. Other apples were still firm and would leave a big bruise.

A teenager picked up a bigger apple that was firm and threw it at Dad. He missed Dad and hit me in the stomach. I was only five years old. I fell to the ground, and I doubled over in great pain. Before anyone knew what was happening, Dad picked up an even bigger apple that was still very green and hard. He was going to hit the young man in the head, but he said something told him not to. Instead, he aimed for his feet. When the apple hit the young man's feet, it knocked him down. Both feet were hit, and he went down with a loud thump.

All this happened within seconds of the apple hitting me. Once Dad had taken revenge on the young man for me, he turned his attention to me. I was still doubled over on the ground, crying and moaning in pain. Everyone came running to see if they could help me. Even the young man came running, apologizing as he came.

Where I was hit could have ruptured my spleen. Dad and Mom were comforting me and checking me over. It took a little time for me to regain my breath. Once I did, and I had stopped crying, they saw that I would be okay. That ended the apple fight for the day. My desire to be with Dad was painful that day. This story shows how my family was always trying to watch over me, but they were unsuccessful at times because some things happen that cannot be foreseen or controlled. We soon went home to Arkansas, after harvest time was over, and it would be Christmas in a few months.

I will tell you the scariest part of my writings. I have never shared the details of the things I am about to reveal. That is what happened the morning our family was almost destroyed. I ask you to stop here and pray for yourself. I know some will close off and just read, but others cannot finish reading this portion. Some will say, "Poor child." Allow yourself to hear your inner child speak to you about the things that have happened in your life. Please. I do not write this section to gain pity or anything else. I write this section to release what I have hidden for more than sixty years. Thank you, Christine, for being there most of the sixty.

This child was raised with a set of very loving and protective parents. He was also loved so very much by his three brothers and his older sister. At times, he could be a real stinker, but they loved him nonetheless. Bubby wanted to be around all of them and do what they did. Once they all were rolling old car rims around the yard, and he thought he could do it too. When he rolled his wheel, it fell over—and almost cut off his toe. Ouch! He went to the doctor, and he was not able to walk for days. Guess who got to carry him around? The younger of the three brothers tried to make him laugh during this time to help him forget his pain. He laughed, but it still hurt. Ouch again!

How often do we find people with memories of their mothers holding them as infants? As an infant, can you look up from her lap and see in detail the love she is expressing on her face? Do you know you are in the safest place you could ever be? Maybe it is just a quick memory, but the memory is still etched in the baby's mind and heart forever. The memory still appears like it was just this morning.

During the Christmas before the fire, the little boy saw a set of toy soldiers in the store window. His brothers and his dad saw it too. He knew he would not be able to have it, but his face was gleaming with excitement at seeing the most marvelous toy ever! Walking away, he turned to look up into his father's face. He saw the disappointment in his dad's face because he would not be able to get it for him. His brothers were beginning to whisper with each other.

Just a few weeks later, it was Christmas. He was excited because it was Christmas, but the most exciting moment was yet to come. Everyone was standing around and smiling for some strange reason. Then they moved aside, and his little eyes could not believe what he was looking at. There on the floor was the army toy set with the truck, trailer, cannon, and soldiers. It was so green and so ready to be played with. His brothers had gotten together and gathered the money to buy it for him. The joy was all over their faces—and it was on his face too. Faster than Superman could leap over a building, the little guy was playing on the floor.

The little guy started every day playing with them at the feet of his brothers while they prepared to go off to do their daily things: one to work and the rest to school. One morning, his middle brother was teasing him by picking up one of the toys and keeping just out of reach. The little guy's first response was to cry out to his Mom to make him give it back. His brother just chuckled and gave it right back. Mom did not have to help; she knew he was playing with Bubby. The little brother just smiled and went back to playing. With each day of his life, he wanted nothing more than to be with them. Each brother had a place in his heart—and so did his sister, his Mom, and his dad. He even had special spots on his face for them to kiss him, an ear, a cheek, a forehead, a nose, a chin, and whatever else was needed.

I want everyone to understand how much this child loved his family. I looked up to my brothers and sister for directions every day. I was loved, and I felt every ounce of love they gave me. Writing this is not as easy as I thought it might be. So many emotions and memories jump out, and I am crying as I write this.

Everything shared during this section feels like it happened this morning. I cannot stop looking at what I see. To some, it would be like a horror film that you cannot stop watching even if you want to. Why am I standing here and watching all this happen? I am a five-year-old who has always trusted the very people dying before my eyes to stop me from seeing. I am watching my loved ones and protectors vanish before my eyes. At that very moment, I knew they were in pain and were never coming back. I was helpless to do anything. There was fire, screaming, and people running—my family running—but I could not move from the chair that was surrounded by fire.

Let me back up a moment or two. Bubby stood in the old chair by the bedroom door, which was at the edge of the living room. In front of the chair was the woodstove where his sister sat to get warm before heading off to school. Bubby's two older brothers were sitting on the couch. The couch was in front of the stove, which was beside the chair and across from the corner of the room. The oldest brother was on the couch, and the second oldest sat at his feet.

Mom was in the kitchen, and Dad was outside. There was a guest in the house, but he was in the bedroom. The youngest of the three brothers stood up from where he was sitting behind the stove to help make the fire burn hotter. He picked up the five-gallon can of kerosene to dash the wood. Friends had told him that was the fastest way to get the fire going. Dad had seen him trying it the day before and had instructed him never to do it again because there were live embers in the stove.

I watched him pick up the can. Inside my head, I wanted to repeat what Dad had told him the day before, but I did not. He opened the wood door in front. I wanted to scream out to stop him. Dad always told us the right things to do—and for a reason—and I soon discovered why Dad had told him not to do what he was doing. He took off the lid so he could dash the kerosene on the wood. As soon as the kerosene touched the coals, it burst into flame. The flame traveled back into the can, causing it to burst into a ball of fire that rocketed across the room to the couch. My older brother had no chance to get out of the way. My middle brother tried to help my older brother. I felt heat all around me, but I was in too much shock to move. The flames had already started burning the chair I was in. I did not feel the flames, but they were there. I watched my brother fighting the fire, but the fire grew too fast.

As soon as the can exploded, I saw my sister run out the door. My younger brother ran into the bedroom. By that time, the whole living room was engulfed in flames. I felt two hands grab me, and I knew they were my mother's hands. I looked around as she carried me to the kitchen. As we passed through the bedroom, I saw someone rolled up in the covers of the bed. Somehow, I knew it was my brother—the one who had started the fire. That was as far as he made it; he chose to stop there and go no farther. That was where he died that morning.

The young man who had spent the night escaped out the bedroom window.

Dad had heard the explosion and ran to knock the back door down, but it was latched from the inside. The door was on the floor near us. Mom dropped me in the kitchen, and I crawled across the door to finish getting out.

Once I was out the back door, my sister led me over to the old chicken coop. We stood there holding hands, and I noticed she was crying and not looking up. I saw my middle brother run out the door. His clothes were all aflame. He was trying to run to the creek to jump in it. Dad grabbed him and pushed him to the ground to tear off his burning clothes.

I heard glass breaking to my left, and I looked to see what was breaking. Mom was trying to get out through the window. She thought she could crash face-first through it. I saw her with such a harrowed look. She was cut and bleeding. She had tried to get the younger brother of the three to safety, but she did not make it. She had to run through the fire, which caused her to come out like my brother, burning.

Dad went to help Mom, and there was so much chaos. Everyone was running here and there. Dad got my sister and me and put us in the car to go find help. The house was burning, and the flames were consuming the house. I sat between Mom and Dad and looked over the back of the seat at my sister, my middle brother, and his friend. I looked out the back window to see the house burning. Even at five, I knew my two brothers had not made it out. The car stopped, and Dad had to open gates for us to get to the highway.

It took forever to get to town. We dropped off the friend, and Dad drove to the state police station on the way to the hospital. One of the troopers came out and drove us on to the hospital. He blew the horn of the car in an SOS rhythm. Other police joined us and led the way.

The doctors and nurses ran out to help. When they took me in, I saw my brother on the bed in the hallway. He was screaming in agony. That was the last time I ever saw him.

They bandaged the burns on my head and hands. My sister and I were loaded into the ambulance to be taken to the children's hospital in Little Rock. They sounded the siren all the way. You probably know how I still feel every time I hear sirens. The smell of smoke brings memories rushing into my mind. There is not a day that goes by that I do not remember it all.

They kept us together, and by the time we were in our room, the bandage on my head had slipped down over my eyes. I could not see anything. My sister kept telling me it was going to be okay, and she tried to encourage me as much as possible. My bandaged hands made it so hard when my face itched.

Dad showed up soon, and I was so glad, but Mom was not there. A very uneasy feeling was beginning to settle into my mind and heart. My sister was crying, and my dad was trying to help us. He told us where Mom was and that he would need to see her. The nurses were so kind and loving to us.

I needed surgery on my face for skin grafts. It took a few days to arrange it all. Dad was there the day I was taken to get it done. They took the skin from my leg, which made it too hard to walk. My sister was released soon, and then I was alone. Another girl was there—my sister had made friends with her—and she tried to comfort me.

During my time there, healing from the surgery, another tragic event that happened. I could not walk because of the surgery on my leg to remove the skin for my face. An air force transit plane exploded over the city. The sound shook the hospital so much that I jumped out of bed and ran for the stairs. I knew to run this time, and I ran toward the closest door I could find. One of the nurses caught me just as I reached the door. I fought her to until I got loose. I wanted to get out of there. She did her best to calm me down and get me back in bed. Another explosion happened. The tanks from the plane had fallen within two blocks of the hospital. I jumped out of bed again and ran for it. The nurse caught me again. I said, "I have had enough. Let me go."

I waited for Dad to come, and it seemed like forever. When he got there, I had calmed down, and everything seemed okay. He talked to me and reassured me that everything was okay. I told him I could walk now. He told me to show him. I tried to get out of bed, but the pain in my leg stopped me. The moment passed, and he smiled at me and helped me lie back down. He was able to take me home soon after that, and some friends drove us home. When we were almost there, my head began to bleed. The bleeding was severe enough that we had to turn around and rush back to the hospital. Dad grabbed me and placed his hand over the place that was bleeding. The hospital was in Newport, and then we went back to Little Rock.

I needed another skin graft. The first graft did not do what it needed to. I had lost lots of blood and needed a transfusion. The male nurse placed my arm on an arm board so I would not bend it, and then he placed the needle in my arm. I watched as the blood flowed down the tube and into my arm.

The nurse tried to comfort me, but it was still hard to lie there and be still. I stayed for a few more days before I got to go with dad to my cousin's house in Little Rock. He finally took me to see my mom. She had been in intensive care that whole time and would be for months. My uncle was there, and he took me to get something to drink. We got lost before we went back to dad. I was so happy to see my dad that I ran to him and hugged his leg like I did every time I was afraid. His touch comforted me, and I felt safe again for the first time in a long time. My mom and I did not get to attend the funeral of my brothers, but I felt like I did because I saw the church and everyone there. Maybe it was because my dad told me about it.

My three brothers were gone, and my mom was not available to see much. She had bandages on every part of her body that I could see. As a little boy, I would wonder if I would lose her too. Cousins and other family members tried to help, but this little guy went inside himself and acted as nothing had happened. The two brothers in the house were placed in the same grave. The one who made it out was placed beside them. My dad took me to see their graves. Later, Dad would place a headstone there with their pictures so all could see what great boys they were. Their ages were seventeen, sixteen, and fourteen. I think they still live in ways inside me. My thoughts resemble them, and Dad told me all about them. They told him that they knew the three of them would not get to go to college, but they had already started planning for me to go. They planned to get one of Dad's kids somewhere in the world.

After I was home, Dad took me to the house that had burned. All that was left were ashes and rubble. The bathtub was in the yard, covering something. When Dad turned it over, I saw the remains of the army set that had been placed there. I was overcome with all that I was seeing, but I could not express my emotions outwardly. I looked for my little red tractor, which had three wheels that I could pedal, but I could not find it. It had also been taken. It would not have burned because it was always in the yard. I was told later that people had come and taken everything left from the fire. Even my brother's boat on the creek had been taken. With everything gone, Dad did his best to make things as normal as he could. He made me some wooden toys to play with, and I played with them every day.

Mom finally made it home. We were all happy to have her home. Things had changed so much from what they had been. The long nights began. Mom had dreams after the fire. Mom would wake us up, screaming from her memories, and the dreams manifested themselves into screams to keep the dogs away from the baby. Many other such dreams would be screamed night after night.

The little guy would replay all the events he had seen that morning, every day, without others knowing what he had seen. Dad took me everywhere he went—even to work. My sister stayed home and cared for Mom. A couple of older ladies lived on our street. The ladies cared for Mom and helped us. The houses were called shotgun houses. When we opened the front door, we could see out the back one. There were three rooms on the side. My sister slept in the front room, and I slept with Mom and Dad in the next one. The kitchen was the last room.

Other people were helpful and gave us couches, beds, dishes, and the like, but the one thing no one could give us was my brothers. Memories of them were all I had. I locked them up tight to keep them safe—and keep the little guy safe. People had taken away all the things I loved, and I was not going to let them take my memories.

I have not told everyone the entire story, and I have been living in fear of them being erased by someone with good intentions. When I was in the second grade, my teacher tried to force me to tell the class what happened. I only told the part of the story about seeing the house on fire. She may have meant well, but she had never talked to me about it privately. You can see how that moment and others like it affected me and made me keep them all locked away.

Dad started building a house on the acre he had bought before the fire. He would spend all his spare time working on it until late at night and many times after he got off work. Weekends were also consumed with getting it done. I would go with him and do whatever a little guy could do. On many nights, it would get dark before he stopped. His brothers and friends would stop by to see how it was going, but they rarely offered much help. I remember them telling him that he would not be able to build it. Even at that young age, I did not believe them. I believed my dad could do anything.

I was with him almost all the time. I had seen him do so many things that he was—and is—my hero. Even in the face of discouraging words, he never stopped. One night he was pounding nails into the roof, which was made of unplaned oak, and he realized he had pounded a nail headfirst into the wood. He thought it might be time to stop. We went home, and I heard him tell sister and Mom about driving the nail headfirst. He would repeat that story many times for the rest of his life. See why I thought he could do anything? Oh! By the way, he did not bend the nail; it drove all the way in.

There are many things I could share about this time, but what would I write in the rest of this book? Living in Zero, the place where the shotgun houses were, offered many moments for me to reflect on. We did not have the freedom we had when we lived in the country. The houses were next to each other, and cars lined up on the side of the road. Other kids were playing all over the place. It was a big difference from just a few months before. I had to learn how to play with other kids, but I'm not sure I ever did. Cousins and family friends would sometimes come over.

Someone affected my life while we were living there. Next to our house, there were two other houses where two widows lived. One would take Mom back to the bedroom to talk. The other would stay with me and become what I would call an incredibly loving grandma-type person. I would hear Mom crying back there. This wonderful lady would distract me from listening and talk to me and play games with me. You have most likely heard of patty-cake. She would sit in her rocker and put me in the other. We would rock back and forth and play patty feet. Bumping the soles of our feet together and just laughing for the longest time. Many a day, she would care for me like that. I never knew much about her family. I just knew she had become my friend at a time when I needed someone like her. These ladies had a frame hanging from the ceiling, which they would let down at times to quilt on it. I would sit for many hours and watch as they and Mom sewed away. They would talk about everything and everybody. Many a quilt was made on that rack and given to others who needed them. A few times, they would even let me sew on it. I think they would redo what I had done later.

We lived there for only a few months before the house was finished. I have so many memories of some of the most loving people I have ever known. We were watched over more than ever before. We were not allowed to be out of sight for more than a few moments.

I would get into trouble while playing with other kids. While not always winning my battles for me, my dad still stood up for me and reassured me that he loved me no matter what. A father and mother's love can never be replaced with anything else. That kind of love helped me make it through the hardest times. Little Bubby had locked himself inside and away from others. He would not cry unless someone hurt him physically. If they did, that person had to pay the price—and they soon learned to avoid the wrath of my dad. Is it any wonder I loved being with him every moment I could?

When we moved to the acre, we could do anything we wanted if we never left the acre. There were no fences, but we were taught where the lines were and to never cross them unless Mom or Dad was with us. It was the first house built in that area, and it was on the corner of city limits. It was the last place before leaving city limits and being in the country, which meant having to walk to school. It was exactly one mile, but it was not uphill or downhill. If we had lived on the other side of the road, the bus would have picked us up. For about twenty minutes a day, in the morning and afternoon, we would be alone as we walked to and from school. We would cross the main highway and cross a small creek with a wooden bridge. If it rained or snowed, we still walked. We walked on cold days, hot days, and spring days that would make anyone want to run for joy.

I was always ready to go home to the acre. I would see Mom and hope that Dad would be there. He worked at the granary, which was on the way home, which made the walk more exciting if I got to see him. Those moments will be shared later. At home, I had things I had to do. I was building imaginary castles with imaginary friends. I might have to watch a cartoon or two on the black-and-white television and watch for Dad because I knew he would be home soon. I had little time to do all I wanted or needed to get done. One imaginary friend was Kong King. He was my best friend and my protector when I faced things that seemed impossible. You can see how I protected little Bubby at times. When we were together, Kong King and others would help me figure things out. I told Dad about him, and he was okay with my friend too.

Before the fire, I asked my dad to switch names with me. He would always call me babe, and I called him Dad. He agreed, and until the day he died, I called him babe, and he called me dad. To avoid confusion, I will refer to him as Dad in these writings.

After changing names, I went to sleep with no problems. I would get into trouble—but never enough to get a spanking. Dad and Mom disciplined me with their love rather than with their hands or a spanking. I never said much to anyone. I was listening, though, to everything. Before the fire, my brothers, sister, Mom, and dad would do my talking for me. Dad, Mom, and my sister kept doing it after the fire. It was not that I had nothing to say. I wanted to say a lot.

I saw more than I thought I had, but I only realized that when I was older. Do you hear someone saying something? Relate or not to the little guy. Listen carefully to what you hear from inside. Is it a smoldering ember or a spark that is ready to ignite? Do you hear laughter, crying, or silence? Will you take time to let God search your life? Are you willing to set yourself free from the wrong done in your life? Are you willing to set yourself free from your childhood memories and all that is going on now? Maybe you will realize that more is gone than you thought.

Take a deep breath and close your eyes. Be quiet and listen. Is there any sound that you hear? Do you hear a small voice? Count down from ten to one and find your place to hear where your next steps will lead. Is there peace where you are right now? Do you still hear nothing? Are there thoughts of running away or running to something unknown? Count from one to ten and breathe again. It is time to rest and help your most inner child rest in your own heart.

CHAPTER 2

BUBBY AND THE ACRE

IT'S TIME TO begin the tales of Bubby's adventures on the acre. Just an acre? What in the world can one do on such a small piece of land?

How exciting to see Dad building the house that would be home for the next fifteen years. I watched him lay the first blocks to set the floor beams on. He set them on the ground where he wanted the house to sit, and then he went back and straightened and leveled them. I watched very closely and walked right beside him as he moved each block. They were the first things to be put on the acre.

I watched as the lumber was brought and placed on the ground. The unplaned oak was rough and uncut. Each had its length, and each cut was done with a handsaw. No power tools were available for Dad. Dad began to nail them together, and within days, I saw the form of the floor. I walked on the beams as any child would do, trying to balance myself as I did. Dad watched, but he kept on working. The house took shape quickly, and the walls went up. I would climb on the ladder behind him once he started the roof. "Careful, Bubby, careful," he would say.

I began to venture around the acre, but there was nothing there except a young boy's imagination. With nothing there to play with, his imagination would feed on the unseen things. He was creating new thoughts and new ideas for what would fill his time there. It was not like he had no training in creating things from nearly nothing. He did not have many toys, and one day, Dad bought home some toys made from wooden boards. He learned that a person could make other things by seeing them and using their imagination to shape a simple piece of wood or anything else that could be molded. I was living in a world without people I had loved, but I still had very fresh memories of those people. Once you feel the love of those you love, peace will follow.

Weeds and grass grew on most of the acre until it was taller than me. The weeds gave me a jungle to find a way to mounds of dirt placed on the acre. Kong King and I would help my other imaginary friends climb the gigantic mountains that rose from the jungle that surrounded them. Many times, we would fight off enemies who wanted to harm us or capture us. We were never captured because we could outsmart anyone in the jungle or desert who might come after us. Many battles were fought to save our kingdom from impending dangers that came from everywhere.

Once I was separated from all my friends, and I was captured. I sent telepathic messages to my commanders, and they would bring the troops to help my getaway. The battle got so intense that I was sweating and breathing so hard. My heart was pounding out of my little chest. Until my troops arrived, I was surrounded by the enemy. I hid among the trees, ran to the foot of the mountain, and hid among the rocks. I received a message asking me where I was. The enemy was coming closer and closer with each moment of daylight. My guns, a piece of wood, were ready to fire until the last bullet. They were not going to take me alive. Everyone knew my mind held secrets that would release dangers to all. These secrets could destroy my life, Bubby's life. The memories he could not tell anyone because they could be shattered or destroyed by them. Firebombs were thrown in my direction without coming too close. Someone wanted these secrets, but who was the mastermind behind the plan? I could feel the earth shaking because they were so close to finding me. Where was my help?

Stop, stay calm, and think. I have gotten out of wicked problems before. Now is the moment for rescue again.

I heard shouting of commands coming from the distance. My commanders were giving orders to surround the enemy and take them hostage. The enemy fought hard to no avail. Soon there were more shouts from the opposing leaders for their army to lay down their weapons. My troops came and stood around me. They were looking at me with relief in their eyes. They were a great group to save me once again from those who had captured me. Once again, the secret would be kept. The enemy would not have the secret that could destroy everyone's hopes for a peaceful life. What was this secret he kept locked away? What would happen if anyone did get it?

On the way back to our secure location, I talked to them about how brave they were to come for me and risk their own lives. Without having to, they told me they would do anything for me—even give their lives for me. What a dedicated band of protectors. Firebombs had burst all around them, yet they came through and carried me out of harm's way.

Once back, we all worked to put away our weapons and equipment. I stood and watched as each knew what they were to do. They cleaned and polished everything so it would be ready for the next moment of need. We all knew there would be more moments like the one we had just been through.

The next day, we planned for and practiced what we would do when that day came. We went through the buildings, valleys, caves, and rivers and rehearsed our plans. The preparation was hard but exciting because each thought came with reassurance. We would also win the next time.

Bubby was older now, and a year had gone by. His friends would never leave his side, and he would not forget them. At night, they were there to comfort when the screams came, keeping the wolves away from the baby. *Lay still, Bubby. It will be okay. The night will pass as the others have, and tomorrow, we will have other great adventures.* It was easy to understand why their friends were there. During that time, Bubby needed such friends.

A few days later, Bubby would drive his homemade building equipment to the location where he would build something great. One new piece of toy or piece of equipment was a dozer. He found a cinder block made of ceramic-type material. It had small holes through it, and one edge was broken. He used a hammer and chipped away at it until it pretty much looked like a dozer without tracks. Yes, it was hard to push; it made him push harder to do what he needed to do. He was so happy and proud of making it all by himself. It became the favorite place while he worked on leveling the ground and making roads to the building site.

So, instead of battles, it would be building the biggest skyscraper that he and his crew could. Bring in the trucks, cranes, and dozers. Make sure the ground is packed and ready for the foundation. It will need to be reliable because it will have to hold this building forever. No earthquake, flood, or storm will ever touch it. We made sure it was the safest one ever built. The mountain turned into something that would stand for the future. My company and I worked so hard to see that everything was placed just like it needed to be. The foundation was placed on the mountain's stone floor. The building started to rise like a mighty giant from the foundation. With each order from the leader, everyone worked hard to do their part. Everyone was working as one. The imaginary skyscraper was coming together. Now, just what did this building look like in the mind of Bubby?

The foundation that could be seen had stones that looked like jelly beans scattered throughout it. Later in life, I discovered there was a riverbed in Little Rock where one could buy truckloads of these stones. The cornerstone was carved to make images of the faces of my friends. Bubby wanted to remember why each one was special to him. The crew was always happy to see him. They would engrave the stone to make images to help everyone in the building smile. The tall doors were made of glass, and anyone could see in and not have to wonder what waited for them. When you looked up, it was almost impossible to see the top. If you wonder how this little guy could imagine this, remember how much time he spent in the children's hospital, taking in everything he saw. That was where he was taken to get better.

Inside, there were places for people to welcome whoever would come. Whatever anyone needed could be found there. Guess what? His friends were working there. They knew what someone needed as soon as they walked in. We are only looking at the entrance to the building.

I could go on and on, but no one would believe he could have such a big imagination. He spent weeks and years working with his crew to finish that beautiful building and space. They all finished just in time because Mom called him in for dinner. The permits would have to wait for another day.

CHAPTER 3

THE ACRE AND DAD

WITH EVERY PLACE where one spends time, there must be something or someone who makes it worth your while. Why else stay there? How can one reason with a child in their understanding and remain objective, sane, grounded, healthy, and okay, okay, we get it? The love that Bubby had for his Dad (Baby) was so great. Dad could leap tall buildings and move anything that stood in his way. He knew how to get people to do things—even when they did not want to do them. So an hour, a day, a year, or years with him on the acre could be very educational in matters untaught in school.

Let us start with him wanting to build a small shed or workplace across the driveway from the house. Granted, the driveway consisted of a gravel bed to drive on if not mud at times. Dad would let me help more than on the house. He took his time to teach me tools and what they did. "Always have a hammer ready to use. There is a certain way to hold it and a way to swing it." He showed me that you could drive a long nail with just two or three hits. After showing me by driving three or four nails, he handed me the hammer and a few nails. I placed the nail on the wood and began to hammer away. I did not think about hitting my fingers. Dad had not hit his fingers. I did not either—that time. I hammered those nails right into the wood. It only took me about twenty hits on each nail. He just watched and grinned. My arm was ready to fall off. I looked up at him, and he reached down and took my hand with the hammer and placed my hand farther back on the handle. He told me that the hammer needed to do the work, not me. I gave a puzzled look, and he slowly explained the reason.

"When a person grabs a thing too close that should be held farther away, you choke it from doing what it was meant to do. Reach for the right spot to work with what you have."

I watched him drive the nail again and watched how he placed his hand on the hammer. He grabbed the end of the hammer, farthest away from the head as he could get. Then he drew back once the nail was started and in place and came down with a mighty force. The nail went in half or more with one hit. Then he drew back as fast as he could, and he came down and hit the nail on its head, driving it in and leaving a mark in the wood of the image of the round-headed hammer.

It was my turn again. I got the nail started, so I would not be holding it when I used the hammer the right way, and I put my hand on the handle where it belonged, at the end. Then I drew back, and with a mighty downward thrust, I gave it all my little hand could do. I missed and hit the board. The nail still stood untouched.

Dad laughed a little and said, "Now hit it."

Believing what he said, I drew back again, and with more aim and determination, I came down with my little force. I was not sure after missing it if I could do it, but to my amazement, I did. It went into the wood about a third of the way. I was so happy, and I was smiling so big.

I aimed again, and down came the hammer. Bang! I hit it, and the nail bent. Feeling a little crushed, I asked why it bent.

He said that the hammer had to be straight with the nail. I had hit it at an angle. Now, what would I do? I thought I could pull it out and start all over with a new nail.

He said that was not the answer. Back then, we did not have the money to replace every nail I would bend. He took the claws of the hammer and straightened the nail somewhat. It was still useable. He finished driving it in to show me it could be done. "Now do it again," he said.

I did, and the nail was started. Bang! I hit it, and it bent again—but not as bad. I worked at getting it straight, and I finished. When he saw that I had done it, he told me what to do and where to nail the rest, and he walked away.

I watched him walk away; he did not look back. I took the next nail and began to drive it into the wood. I finished that board and placed the next board. You might wonder how such a little guy could do this. It was not that I was building a house. It was a simple exercise to give me skills for later in life. Without me knowing what he was doing, he was giving me skills that would help me in areas of my life. Some of the nails went in straight, and some had to be corrected as I hammered away. I was not as fast as he was, but I did it anyway. I was not thinking about being fast. I was thinking about doing what he told me to do. I was so curious about what he did. I wanted to be like him and do what he did all the time. There would be other tools that he would teach me to use and other things I would build. The skyscraper was imaginary, but now my imagination was taking shape in real life. Every day, I would find something to do and work on.

He taught me how to replace the tools and clean them to be ready for the next time. His motto was this: "Take care of the tools, and they will be there ready to take care of what you need to do the next time you need them." All the tools had their places, and if they were not in the right place, you could tell just by looking at the others. Life is that way also. Take care and notice where everything needs to be, and the pieces will be right when it is time to live.

The acre was right next to the town airfield. I watched every day as crop dusters would take off and land across the road. I was amazed at how they would travel down the field and lift off the ground at a certain speed. They were so noisy, and I can still recognize the sound when I hear it. The plane would unload what it was spraying and then return for another load. Day after day, I would watch this beautiful thing happen. I asked Dad if I could build me a plane, and he helped me find some old lumber and used nails. He went back into the house and left me to my imagination to bring it to life.

I planned it all out and laid the pieces on the ground how they were to be. The first nail went into the wood. It would be made of two-by-fours and one-by-fours. The primary wing was a one-by-six. I had no wheels yet, but that would come soon enough—plank on a plank and nail to each place needed. Days later, I finished it—and it sort of looked like a plane. There was a problem. How was I going to make it fly? Dad gave me no clues; he had no interest in planes. It took me a few days to work something out. I thought about how I could get it off the ground. I found some planks that would work, and I placed each end of the top of the plank of something tall and the other end on the ground. I placed the plane on at the bottom and worked on getting it to the top. Push, I got it to the top, and down it would come. I had to get something that would hold it there until I could get on it. A little piece of rope to tie it with, a slipknot next, something Dad had taught me how to tie at another time. How to keep it there until I had tied it was the next problem.

All the problems were solved, and it was time to get on and fly away. I was ready; it was the moment to see how it would feel to fly. My feet were in place, and my hands were ready to pull the rope to start my journey into the air. No one was there for my first fight. I pulled the knot on the rope—and away I went. I was flying. I lifted off, and my speed increased. I was high up, and I could see everything below me. I felt so proud of what I had done. I flew so far and so high. I did not want it to end. The air was in my face and blew my hair. The force was fantastic. It seemed like forever, and I could have stayed up forever. The flight lasted a second or two.

Bang! The nose of the plane hit the ground. The force almost threw me on my face, but I had braced myself with my feet. I had done what I wanted. I pushed it back up the planks, and I got ready for my next flight. The next day, the neighbors came over, and I showed them my plane. Wow! They wanted to try it too. We had lots of fun with it. A second or two is a lifetime when we enjoy it the right way. Later, I found wheels for it. With a short rope, I was able to pull it with someone on it—and then they would pull me. The flights lasted longer, and the acre became our landing field.

Thanks, Dad, for teaching me how to use the hammer and for letting me use the hammer and other tools. The right tools and a good imagination can send you off to worlds unknown. Every day is a reminder of days gone by that taught me how to overcome the limits that keep a person from flying higher than ever before.

CHAPTER 4

TEACHING BUBBY
HOW TO SWIM

JUST BECAUSE SOMEONE tells you an old fable does not make it true. Other factors can change the outcome. The summer before the fire was a hot one—as they all are in Arkansas. My family would cool down by swimming in the rice canals. My family, friends, and cousins would go and make a full afternoon of it. The canals were made of dirt levies that were mostly around six feet deep. The water was cold, not cool, and it was pumped from deep underground by big pumps. The pipes were anywhere from six to twelve inches across. The pumps would have so much force that the water would shoot many feet out of the end of the pipe.

The water would run through the canals until it reached where the farmers needed it to go, and then it was piped into the fields for the rice. It was as clear as could be, and it was even drinkable. Many creatures enjoyed the abundant water. Animals, fish, and snakes could be found around the edges and in the water. It was amazing to look at the canal. It would wind around and through where it needed to go. They had been there so long that trees had grown up beside them in many spots. You would know where people got in because there would be a bare spot of dirt or mud on the levy. The clay soil could become very slick from all the water dripping off people as they got in and out.

We would hear the usual sounds that people make when they are swimming and having fun, and one shouts this joy and another that one.

It was deep enough to drive in headfirst without any danger. Everyone would be safe because before anyone got in, someone would check beneath to see if anything had changed since the last time we were there. The water ran along the canal at a good flow, but it was not fast enough to pull you under like a river. For the most part, it was a very safe place to cool off and get clean for the day.

While we were there, we would have something to eat and drink. After all, it was a country family outing. By the way, there were no paved roads. They were all dirt roads we traveled to get there. Without a care in the world, it seemed like everyone had fun and enjoyed themselves. It would feel so good to have fun, get cool, and enjoy all the family time. After a hard week of work in the fields, it was a good time to relax. Mom would sit on the bank, not getting in, just cooling her feet at the edge of the water. My brothers were dunking each other in the water, and my sister was playing close to Mom. I was close to Mom as well. Dad was having fun with the older boys in the deeper water. He was a big kid too, at times.

We saw some cousins and friends. They said, "How are you doing? How is the water?"

We said, "Come on in. The water is great."

Splash! Someone else jumped in. Splash! They were all talking about their week and how hard they had worked. The fields were dusty, and we needed rain—but not too much. The work would be chopping cotton, cultivating crops, tending cows, or mending fences. It did not matter at that point because everyone was there to relax, have fun, eat, cool off, and enjoy each other's friendship and company.

I can only guess what led to me to not learn how to swim. For the rest of my life, I would hear the same story from Dad. He would tell the story of how Indians would teach their children to swim. He told us that if one of their children could not swim, someone in the tribe would take them to the deepest part of the river. Once they were there, the older one would pick up the younger one who could not swim and cast them in and watch them learn. They had to be fast learners—or they would sink. He never really finished the story because the one in the water would swim. I do not remember him telling me what happened if they did not learn.

When I was learning how to swim, no one was ready for the outcome. I was only five, and everyone protected me. I had no fear of water since I had no reason to be afraid. My family protected me from fire and water, which could be so deadly. Everyone was having fun and not watching me too closely. The youngest of my three brothers was taking care of me. He held my head up out of the water, and I was doing fine. Splash. Someone jumped, and I got a little water in my face, but it was okay. Somehow, my brother had me in the deepest area of water. I was not worried because he could swim like a fish. He told me it was time to learn to swim. He dropped me and swam away. Instead of flailing my arms and screaming, I just folded up my legs and sank straight to the bottom.

That part of the experience might seem unbelievable. As I sank deeper and deeper, I had my eyes open. I was not at all afraid. My knees were folded up, and I settled on the bottom of the canal. It was so peaceful; the water muffled the voices and noise that came from the top. I could see the legs of everyone as they walked by; they did not know I was there. Time seemed like it was suspended. What were only a few moments seemed like an hour or more. I even saw a couple of little fish swimming by, and I loved watching them. Now I know they were perch. They were big enough to eat, but it was amazing to watch them underwater.

I noticed the legs and feet moving faster, and I could hear screaming. That was not fun, but the voices were muffled. I began to sense something was wrong, but I did not know I was missing. Mom had a scream that always told me something terrible had happened. No one knew where I was—just that I had disappeared into the water. I saw the legs of my brother, the middle brother of the three, coming toward me. I saw his hands reaching down, and then I felt them wrapping around my body. My face was pushing up through the water, and I could see the top of the water getting closer. As soon as my face hit the air, I do not remember anything else until I was revived.

I can only tell you what I was told in the years to follow. I had drowned. There was no air in my lungs. They had filled with water. In those days, no one took first aid or learned how to resuscitate a person who had drowned. I had two heroes that day: my middle brother and my dad. Dad took me by my feet and swung me around and around, forcing the water from my lungs. Once the water was all out, I began to breathe again. I remember coming back to life and feeling the happiness of everyone there. The emotions I still feel every time I remember this part is deep-seated within my memory. I was unable to express how I felt. We would go back to the canal at times—but with a very watchful eye on Bubby.

There were lessons behind the events of fire and water in the life of the little five-year-old boy. He learned what they could do to him, but he did not become afraid of them. The fire became the place to investigate. Maybe it was a focal point of trying to find what had been lost in it. It was always a mystery to watch the flames dancing and growing too hot. I watched how it started and how it continued to consume whatever it touched. The smoke and the flames were not the fire. They were the after-effects. The fire was found in what was burning. Spraying water into the flame and smoke made them dance around the water and play even more. Spraying the water onto what was being consumed would make the flame and smoke go away. Learning that gave me the perspective that all fires have a point of burning. The best way to put out a fire is to remove or smother the point of the fire.

While one cannot be embraced by fire without being consumed, you can be embraced by water and feel secure. You must learn how to hold your breath when your face is submerged or have something to help you breathe. I feel so at peace when I am under the water, but having something that helps me breathe underwater is better. When I went scuba diving, it was such a feeling of peace. I was always mindful of how much air was left in the tanks. The water magnified objects and sometimes distorted them. It was a whole new world to study. When I sink into the depths of the water, I have the same peace as the five-year-old. When I come up out of the water, I remember what is happening.

The fire and the water are different in that one consumes—and the other embraces. Am I afraid of fire and water? I do not think so. I have learned what they do and the meaning behind their actions. In Oklahoma, I even joined a volunteer fire department. In six months, there were ninety-six fires to respond to. I was called out for every one of them. Each time, with the other firefighters, the fire would be overcome.

During the flood days of early spring, I would be asked to check areas where the flood was affecting people and the land. I know how to handle a fire that needs to be controlled. Water needs to do what it is going to. Life is that way also. You must know when to put something out or let it run its course. Being five years old does not make a child a child. Deep in the mind of the child is curiosity. The child wants to understand all that happens and why it happens. Encourage them and help when you can.

Keep an eye on the little guy and help him be safe. He will have the freedom to work things out for a lifetime without the fear that will burn or choke him from becoming what he or she was meant to be.

CHAPTER 5
SISTERS ON THE ACRE

THERE ARE PEOPLE you might fight with, but love finds a way to captivate your heart. Certain people will always hold a special place in your heart.

Have you ever loved someone but did not understand them very much? Bubby had two sisters who he loved so very much. One he fought with like cats and dogs, which only brought them closer together. The other was eight years younger, and he tried his best to watch over her. Bubby's sisters were twelve years apart. The older one had gone through the fire with him. The younger one came two years after the fire. The older one was the only girl out of the five kids until after the fire. He always thought they were the favored kids of Mom and Dad, but Mom and Dad made us all their favorites. Whatever any of the three wanted, Mom and Dad did their best to get it for them—even when there was only enough money to put food on the table.

For clarification, in this part of my writing, Sister is my older sister, and Little Sister is the younger one. Sister watched over me when we would go to school. She was there at the drop of a hat when the teachers could not handle me. I was traumatized at school many times when I first started. The teachers would have to get her to help calm me down. When she came, and I saw her, I knew things would be all right. Even in the hospital, she was the one to calm me down and tell me that everything was going to be okay. I was a handful in those days, and no one could understand me except the ones who had gone through it with me.

She and I would walk the mile to school every day except the days when Dad was off work and came to pick us up. That was the longest mile you could ever imagine. At the time, she stood much taller than me, and I looked up to her. We did physically fight, and Mom and Dad would let us wrestle until it got out of hand. She would do things that made me laugh without even trying. She would do my talking for me. She would boss me around. I did not like that, but I let her anyway. Does that not sound like a loving brother and sister? She had her hands full most of the time, trying to watch out for me. Listen to this. I was still her little brother. Big sisters are supposed to watch over little brothers, and little brothers are supposed to resent it. She would have friends over, and I would do my best to get in on the fun. I would soon give up and go out to run around the acre. I could hear them laughing and having fun when I went past her room, and I wondered what they were doing.

Kong King and the others would keep me entertained during that time. Some of what I will tell you in this chapter comes from a few years. I know you have that figured out, but I said it anyway. On other days, she would spend time doing things and playing games with me on the acre.

Then Little Sister came into our lives. We were all excited when we knew there was going to be a new baby in our house. I thought brother, and my sister probably thought sister. Well, I got a little sister. She was a pretty baby. Both of my sisters grew up to be beautiful women. Little did anyone know that I was happy to have her in our family. I never said much, and even Little Sister spoke for me too, crying a lot at first. You know how babies are.

Sister quickly became a little mama for Little Sister. I wonder if anyone thought she was the mother. Sister could get her to stop crying fast, and that was okay with me. I did not have much to do with her as an infant. When she began to walk, I took more interest in being around her. I began to take on a bigger brother role in her life. I went out and played on the acre, and then I would come in and just look at her in Sister's or Mom's arms.

The three of us—Sister, Little Sister, and I—had lots of fun at times. I would go with Dad a lot more, and I was not around her as much. Later in life, I heard that she did not know she had a brother because I was not around that much.

When she was learning to rock in the rocking chair, she tipped it over—and it came down hard onto her head. I was on the floor across from her, and when I saw her falling, I rolled across the floor to catch the back of the chair before it hit her. She was on her knees, and she gave me a look that I will always remember. She seemed to understand that I had helped her. No one else saw what happened—only that she had fallen out of the chair. I took care of her when she and I went outside, but I learned later that Mom was watching us all the time. There were times I wanted to be alone, but she was there. I was not as patient as I should have been. She always got to me, and I would let her stay around. She still gets to me to this day. They both do—even now—but I do not tell them.

I had two roles at the same time: little brother and older brother. One to pester and one to be annoyed—what a wonderful world we lived in. It was good to have them. The love we lost when we lost our brothers was not lost between us. (Am I looking through rose-colored glasses? Hey, I am only five to eight years old. I can do that.)

During that time, I slept in the bed with my dad. Little Sister slept with Mom in another bed beside ours. Sister had her room and bed. Still, it was a single wall separating all of us. This was the arrangement we had for some time. I did get too big and finally got my bed. I was put in a corner of the room that was supposed to have been the closet. No comments please. I was still in the room with Mom and Dad.

At night, I could still hear all of them with the sounds they made. One was snoring, one was crying at times, and another was having bad dreams, and so forth. Once I was asleep, I would dream of everything you can imagine a small boy having who had an active imagination. I had no idea that I would grow up dealing with dreams and trying to understand what they mean. They were exciting dreams then—and they changed my mood for the most part.

When we were home, Sister would help Mom get things ready to cook and do laundry. Changing diapers was something else she did. I was never asked to—and I did not want to either. When that happened, it was time to go out and be creative. I could tell when it was all done by the sounds that came from the house. That was in the days when people used cloth diapers. Store-bought diapers were not known in our house. I do remember the smell. Maybe that explains why I can tell if a baby needs changing from at least thirty feet away—time to move on.

Sister and I got a job picking cotton in the field across the road from the house. We showed up for work early in the morning. I had seen it done many times and thought I knew how. She had her sack, and I had mine. Those bolls of cotton had some very sharp points that would stick your fingers faster than anything you've ever seen. You were to get all the cotton out of the bolls without leaving any fiber from the cotton. If you left the smallest fiber, that was called "goose necking your cotton."

Noontime came, and we gathered around. The granary where Dad worked was on the other end of the field from the house. Dad was there while we picked cotton. When it was time to get back to picking cotton, the owner called us all together to talk to us. He handed me money for what I had picked that morning and told me to leave and not come back. My sister got to keep working. I did not understand why I could not work anymore. Then I was told I was goose necking too much. My fingers did not feel like it. They were hurting so much from getting stuck all morning. It did not bother me because I ran to where Dad was and told him I could not go back to picking cotton. Not going back to pick cotton meant more time with Dad at work.

"How about playing with Little Sister outside of the house on the acre?"

I was not sure how to at first. She was much younger, and I had learned to play by myself. I tried different things to please her. This or that did not work—why? The best way to find out was to ask her what she wanted to do. She was able to tell me. Not long after discovering this new concept of play, we were able to play together. Many times, dolls were involved. Other times, she just wanted to be with me and go where I wanted to go. In the background, Kong King and the group were telling me what to do to please her. They were listening better than I was. Mom was always mindful of where we were and what we were doing without me knowing it. We both had lots of fun. Little Sister loved our pets, and when we were outside, they were always with us. She learned to take care of them, and she still takes loving care of her pets.

There were times we all would embarrass Mom. I did as a little child, and the rest would do it too. I still remember those days, and Little Sister does too. Mom would run after us, and we would run away from her. When I did, I thought it was very funny, and when Little Sister did, I thought it was very funny too. Years later, Mom would tell the stories of what we did to others to embarrass us. It did not work.

Always embrace the love of family. You may not feel loved at all times, but it should never cause you to stop loving. Family cannot be replaced. The experiences as family, brothers, sisters, Mom, and Dad are etched on stone—and carved in the woods—forever.

CHAPTER 6
BUBBY'S FAMILY

EVERYONE HAS DNA that affects them their entire lives. Moms and dads and brothers and sisters have the most influence on us while we are growing up. Family is what we were made to be—embrace your past. Let me share the chronicles of my past. Who are we? Are we the sum of all who came before us? Each person has within their life the makeup of the people who gave their DNA to make us who we are. Truths and lies are part of who we are. The good, the bad, and whatever comes next is in us. What we do with it is up to us. No two people are alike. Even twins will have some differences somewhere. I am me, and you are you. Are you not happy with that?

Dad's and Mom's family trees are full of stories and legends. Dad's father was Charlie Woods, but that was not his birth name from what we all heard. At the age of fifteen or sixteen, he left home, never to return, and changed his name. He chose the name from a dictionary of names. After my grandmother died and everybody had gone through everything she had, I was permitted to look in an old trunk that had only a few pieces of paper in it by then. I looked through the papers in the trunk and found a page that had been ripped out of a dictionary of famous names. On the page, a name was circled in red ink. The name was Charles Woods, and it belonged to a general of the Confederate Army during the Civil War. I guess that was how he got his name. There was more to the article, but it did not pertain to my grandpa. Dad said he never told him where he came from. There was always speculation and many rumors about his life. Some included that he was the son of a rich man who owned a logging company in Oregon, and another was that he came from Missouri. There was a time that his name was used to acquire land in California to obtain logging rights. He never claimed the land after the logging was done, and the state claimed the land to make parks. We may never know, but what we do know is how he raised his family.

Charlie and Mammae (Grandma) had eleven children. One died in early childhood. There were seven boys and three girls—each as unique as could be. Dad seemed to be the closest to his oldest brother and looked like him. Grandpa died in his fifties and left them to make their way in the world. They looked after each other. They had friends join them to work and make it through the Great Depression. They were known as the Woods gang. Most people were afraid of them, but there was no need to be. They would defend anyone who needed their help.

Dad and a couple of his brothers were almost sold into slavery. When they saw what was happening, they escaped and went home. The stories my dad told would fill a large book if I told them all.

Grandma, Dad's mom, was a fiery little lady who nobody messed with. Grandma's mother was a Cherokee woman who lived to be 115 years old. Grandma would take a switch to the boys without hesitation—even after they were grown. She loved her snuff and whiskey. She lived to be ninety-six or ninety-seven years old. Two of her sons would live with her most of their lives. My uncles were always ready to get together with Dad and family on weekends. Their sisters would join in sometimes. The one who joined us most of the time was named Bessie. Everyone needs a Bessie in their lives. I never called them Grandma, Uncle, or Aunt. I called them by their first name—just as Dad did. I was never told to call them by any other name or title. It was not disrespectful; that was just how our family handled things. You were who you were. Each family had lots of kids, and the cousins got to play while the adults told stories about the past. I spent most of my time wrapped around Dad's knees, not wanting to do much with the others. Most of them were older than me anyway.

Mom's family had two brothers and three sisters. There were also two half sisters who I never met. Her dad, my grandpa, died before I was born. Grandma was the daughter of a Cherokee Indian.

I did not know my two uncles from Mom's side very well. I was named after one of them. I got to know her sisters well, especially the oldest one. The older sister would spend more time with Mom. The youngest lived in Little Rock, which was about ninety miles away. Grandma was not too easy to be around by the time I got to know her. She had had a stroke and could not get around particularly well; she used a cane to walk. The cane was used as a method of making kids stay in line and do what kids should do, and we gave her lots of room. She came to live with us in the last years of her life. Mom and her brother moved a small RV trailer in and made her home there on the acre. I still remember her calling out during the night for Mom to come and check on her. With Mom having her dreams and grandma calling out, there was not much sleep.

I was a picky eater. When the families would get together, I think it was a game of who could get me to eat. If anyone had graham crackers, they won. Some of Dad's brothers moved to California. Dad and Mom thought about it, but in the end, they stayed on the acre. That was the best decision they could have made. Many of my adventures I will share would not have happened if we had moved to California.

Dad and his brothers were considered to be a gang in their day, but they were not out to harm anyone—and grandpa had raised them to be very respectful to others. A newscaster on the local television station commented one day that there were only two things he feared growing up—and one of them was the Woods gang. Dad heard it and told me that if the man had known them, he would not have had any fear, but when people see that many young men, they become afraid. People have the same fear today when they see boys together.

The things Dad told me about how he grew up and how he seemed not to fear anything or anybody only affirmed my trust in him and taught me how not to fear many of the things people fear today. Grandpa Woods sounded like a man who was determined to raise his family in the right way. Grandma was one of his significant challenges in life from what Dad told me. Dad said that Grandpa would always say that Grandma was half Indian and half bulldog. When I asked why, he said, "Grandpa said that when she was not on the warpath, she was sitting around growling." If you had known her, you might have agreed. While she did not seem to care for our grandkids like a normal grandma might, you would still understand she loved each one.

Grandpas and grandmas should be a big part of their grandchildren's lives. They should know how to love them and help them not fear the world they live in. I grew up not knowing what it was like to have such grandparents. On the other hand, I had many older friends of Mom and Dad who became like grandparents to me. The older lady in the fire chapter was like that to me. Her name was Mrs. Baggily. We live in a world that needs safe older people who can give a child the grandparenting that will help them have a life filled with love.

What can be said of aunts and uncles? Aunts and uncles can make the best friends a nephew or niece can have. Dad and Mom's relationship with their brothers and sisters helped me with them. I will not bore you with all of them. Dad's closest brother was the one who Dad talked with most. They would call each other every night—even if they were together all day. They were almost twins, but they each had their own way of raising their kids. This uncle's kids were older than me, and I did not get to hang out with them. I was only known as little Bubby.

This uncle and a couple of the other uncles would talk with just me at times. I enjoyed being around them and talking. They never talked up to me or down to me; we were on a first-name basis, after all. Aunts were the same way. When I went to eat at their houses, I would not need to look for graham crackers. One aunt scared me one time when we went to visit her. I had not been around that aunt much at all. When we arrived at her home, she ran out of the house and began to hug everyone. I locked the doors and stayed in the car. That was too much for me to handle. I did get out when she promised not to hug me like that. I am sure I hurt her feelings, but later in life, we did hug.

Dad was forty-one years old by the time I was born. Maybe being older and already having raised the older ones made him see things differently for me. He was always watching after me and over me. If someone hurt me, that person suffered the wrath of Dad. Mom and Dad never spanked me. They did not have to; all they had to do was look at me a certain way, and I would be hurt worse than if I had been spanked. They told us that if we ever did something wrong, we should try to outrun them and not get a spanking.

I once did something that upset Mom, and I knew it. I ran, and she chased me. I ran to the elm tree in the front yard and climbed it to get away. However, that was the second problem because we were not to climb trees. She stood there looking up at me, crying and saying what she was going to do when I came down. "You know what you did, Bubby?"

"Yes, Mama, I do. I am sorry."

"I am still going to spank you."

Looking down with tears in my eyes, I said, "I know, Mama."

She went back inside the house.

I stayed up in the tree for a little longer. When I went down to get my just rewards, she grabbed me and hugged me. We both laughed, and all was at peace once more.

Another time, I did something else that was stupid when Dad was there. I bolted out of the house faster than lightning, thinking I had made it out safe. I looked back only to discover he was right behind me, running after me. I never dreamed he could run that fast. I ran over mounds of dirt, through tall grass, and under low-hanging limbs. Nothing seemed to slow him down. I thought I could make a getaway if I could jump the fence at the edge of the acre. I jumped with ease—only to discover that he did too. He caught me, and he landed on my back. He sat there for a moment before turning me over. My thoughts were all about what was going to happen to me. When he turned me over, Dad was laughing so hard. He had caught me, and that was his prize and punishment for me. We got up, climbed over the fence, and laughed as we went back into the house. Mom was laughing just as hard as we were.

Let me spend a minute here to paint a picture of my family. I will start by describing my dad and my brothers. The extended family always referred to Dad and my brothers as the Cartwrights. Dad was Ben, the dad, Leon, the older brother, Adam, Earl, the middle brother was Hoss, and Wilson was Little Joe, which pretty much tells you what they looked like and how they acted. You could not have found a better match for any of them. Their personalities matched almost perfectly to each of them. If you have never seen Bonanza, it is time to watch reruns. Dad always had a gentle answer for the boys and did what was right. Leon would be the thinking and quiet worker, Earl was the bigger of the three and the protector who would pick up the fight for the others, and Wilson was the one who was fast for trouble and ready to get into fights. He was also a great hunter.

Before going to school, Wilson would go hunting every morning and bring something home for dinner that night. Earl helped Wilson at times when he picked a fight. My sister, my mom, and I were part of the family that the others watched over.

Dads, moms, aunts, uncles, and cousins all make up what should be an excellent place to grow up and become what we were meant to be. If everyone plays by the same rules and the right rules, we all will be fine. You learn that everyone is different. You learn to accept them for who they are and not judge. There are no poor or rich relatives. Everyone is loved and cared for just as they are.

CHAPTER 7

SEASON'S GREETING

BEWARE OF YOUR timing when telling the truth. It could be told sooner rather than later. The truth needs to be told, but make sure the one who needs to hear the truth is not fragile. People may need time to process what they have heard before they can accept the whole truth. When I was seven, I was told a truth that I think could have waited. Even an hour would have made the difference of a lifetime. It was Christmas time. Christmas after the fire was always hard on all of us. It was a time to remember those who were lost more than a time of celebration. Christmas was the grandest time for me. I still held happy memories and wanted to hang onto them as best I could.

In the small town I grew up in, an event happened every year. The fire department would have Santa ride on the truck through town and let kids ride with him. I had imagined my moment riding in the fire truck with him. I was looking forward to what that Christmas meant to me. Not much was said at home about what we would do for Christmas. At school, I had heard about the fire truck ride with Santa and how excited all the other kids were. Some had done it every year, and their stories were so exciting to hear. With my imagination, you can only guess what a fantastic moment I had built up in my mind. If my imagination could make Kong King a master monkey, just think what making friends with Santa could do.

I asked Dad if I could ride the fire truck with Santa, but he would not answer me. For weeks, I would ask if I could see Santa. About two days before, he finally told me that I could. It was enough time to tell the other kids I was going to go for a ride. It also gave me enough time to plan what I would do on the truck and what I would say to Santa. This big man who loved children and gave them gifts would be where I could reach and touch him. The toys I was dreaming of were the kind that only Santa could get for me. I knew that we did not have the money to buy much. This way, I could get what I dreamed of. It happened once, and it could happen again. The first time, I knew it was my brothers who bought the army set for me, but Santa was still a part of Christmas.

The night before, I was so excited. I do not think I slept that much because my little heart and mind were racing each other. I dreamed of running up to the fire truck and Santa seeing me. He would help me climb aboard, and off we would go. Sirens were screaming and announcing to everyone that we were coming down the road. Ho Ho Ho! I would be laughing all the way. All the children would be screaming at the tops of our lungs with excitement and joy. The toys I had in mind were trucks, machines, and army figures. A BB gun would be nice also. I had one before the fire, and it would be nice to have one again. Dad was teaching me to shoot the real gun, a twenty-two, and I was still hanging on to memories of a loving time as much as I could. Staying associated with pre-fire memories of happiness would help me cope.

The morning came, and I was ready to go. I got up early and dressed for the day. It was a little cold, and I got a coat and waited until it was time to go. I waited outside for Dad to call me, and then I went back inside to see if he was ready. He and Mom would say that it was still too early, and I would run outside for a little while. I noticed Dad and Mom talking about something and getting quiet when I came around, but I did not pay attention to what they were saying to each other.

On the way to town, Dad seemed quieter than usual. He would usually talk to me and ask what I was going to do. I had my mind set on what was about to happen, and I did not say much either. I did not know what to expect either. I only knew I was going to see Santa in person for the first time. We only lived a mile from town, but it seemed longer.

We finally got to town, and Dad parked where he always did. It was near the store where we bought our food. He parked five blocks away from where the firehouse was. We got out of the car, and we were about to start walking. Dad stopped me, got down to my level, and looked me in the eye. "Now, Bubby, I need to tell you something. I know you are headed to see Santa Claus. There is no real Santa Claus. That will be a man in a suit dressed like him. There has never been one. I need you to know before you get on the fire truck with the man in the suit. Now, let us go so you can see him and ride the fire truck."

I was stunned and did not know what to do. No Santa Claus, I thought. My eyes filled with tears, but Dad was holding my hand and leading me along. Blocks turned into miles, and thoughts of all kinds ran through my head. No Santa Claus?

As we got closer, I could hear the sirens screaming and people talking loudly. I saw the fire truck pulling up to stop where I was to get on. It was loaded with kids, and they were getting off. All of them were so happy and cheerful. I saw them running to their parents and shouting about what had just happened. I heard a few kids talking about how they got to talk to Santa. Then they all moved out of the way for the next group to get on, which would include me. By that time, I was ready to leave and just go home. I had already heard enough, and the siren was making me uneasy. Remember, I had been in the ambulance just two years before which used the sound of the siren the whole trip. Dad walked me over and got me on the truck, and I could have walked closer to sit by Santa. I sat as close to the back as I could without falling off. Two firemen on the back spent the whole trip watching over us. All I could do was look at where the fire truck had been. I did not turn to look at the man in the suit. I still had tears running down my cheeks. Using my sleeve, I dried them off as best I could.

(Is this ride ever going to be over?) The truck went down this street and then that street. I never knew that town had so many streets. Every time the sirens blasted, I would cover my ears. My thoughts were going everywhere, but they were not on the ride. (Can I please get off now?) Out of the corner of my eye, I saw the truck turning, and we were back where we started. I was the first one off since I was in the back. Dad was there, and I ran to him. He took me by my hand, and we walked away. He asked me how I liked it.

I did not answer his question. I said, "Can I go home now?"

He tried to talk with me a little more, but I was silent all the way home. Once home, I jumped from the car and ran to where I could play by myself. He went inside the house. Suppertime finally came, but I did not eat much. Soon, I was ready for bed.

I know it was hard for Dad to do what he did. I knew it then also. Dad had told all the kids about Santa in somewhat the same fashion. I should not have been hurt like I was. I think every kid knows there is no Santa; we just do not want to admit it. Believing a lie is sometimes more comfortable.

After the fire, Christmas was never the same. Christmases were always hard for all of us. We held on to whatever we could to survive the season. It did not take too many days to get past the news he gave me that day. I still had my dad, and he was real. Dad and Mom were my heroes. Besides, after I grew up, I got to drive fire trucks. However, I did not sound the siren as much.

Telling the truth is sometimes hard, especially when you know someone's hopes are based on a lie. I have tried to be sensitive to people when I tell the truth to them about something that has been untrue their whole lives. Everyone needs to know the truth. It will help them find a solid footing in life. Learning that there was no Santa helped me be careful about believing in just anything because someone said it was true. I did not become a cynic. I believe people have pure motives most of the time. I do, however, research what I believe and why I believe it. I know that what I believe cannot be diluted by fire trucks and men in red suits. If someone tells me that someone or something is not true, I will look for what is true. Thanks, Dad, for having the courage to tell your little seven-year-old the truth. I now know it hurt you as much or more than it did me.

When people are confronted with the truth, give them time to react. Like the inner child, it takes time to understand and accept what is best over the old that was not good. My question for myself and you is this: "Do you hear crying or laughter now?"

CHAPTER 8

OFF THE ACRE FOR A NIGHT WITH DAD

MANY TIMES, A child will go to work with a parent. Maybe it is not always a wise decision. Later in life, it can prove to be a life lesson that helps that child through rough times. This chapter will not be the only one of its kind. On the contrary, it is just the first. Dad worked during harvest time at the local granary. His job included any number of things to do. The one that would scare a person the most was having to climb to the top of the silos to check how the grain was doing. Was it going into the right bins? Was it dry enough? He would be at work by seven and work until seven the next morning. Many nights, he would take me with him, and I would stay all night. Many would cringe at that point, thinking about how dangerous that was back in the days of no cell phones or even party line phones.

Many nights, I would go with him and sleep the next day. Maybe I got to go so I would sleep while he did. Every night was a new adventure for me. Everyone had gotten used to me being there. On the wall of the grain office, there was an old-timey phone. In that area, the grain was checked and transferred. A person would have to pick up the receiver and crank the handle on the side of the phone to get the operator. She was always there to answer. I guess I had seen them use the phone. One night, I was left alone in the small area with the phone. It was high enough I could not reach it. Do not tell me I cannot do anything. I am my father's son. I realized the bench would move and would be the right height to give me the reach I needed to use the phone.

I opened the door to see if anyone was coming. Nope. I jumped on the bench and grabbed the earpiece. After cranking the handle and listening, I heard the prettiest, kindest voice talking to me. The operator asked me how she could help me. It was midnight by then. This shy little boy began to talk to her. She would ask me so many questions, and I did not know to tell her anything but the truth. She never asked for my dad or a grown-up to talk to. We would talk for the longest time—or until I thought I heard someone coming.

I would sing songs to her, including "She Will Be Coming around the Mountain When She Comes," and many other songs that I knew. I usually was not able to talk without an impediment. When I talked with her, it all went away. Many nights, I waited for Dad to leave and do his job. She always sounded happy to have me ring that phone. Night after night, I learned how to use that phone, but good things can only last so long. One night, Dad was not leaving, and the time for me to call was getting close. I asked him if he was going to check on things like he always did. He said he would in a moment. I guess I was being too obvious. I kept asking what the sounds were that I was hearing. "Don't you need to check on that in case something is wrong?"

He played along and told me he heard it too. Out the door he went, and I did not even wait for the door to close, but I should have. I had just called, and we were starting our nightly meeting when the door banged open—and Dad stepped through the door. The cat had swallowed the canary, and there was no getting it back. I looked at him, and he looked at me. My look was I am caught, and his look was I caught you. He asked what I was doing, and I told him I was talking to the lady. He took the phone, and I lost my midnight date.

Moments in time encourage us to do more. How about that little guy who was so shy he would not talk to anyone unless Dad, Mom, or Sister was talking for him. At night, I talked for myself to someone I did not know and had never seen.

He kept his eyes on me and watched for my next adventure. He asked questions to tease me. "Do I need to go and check something?" I never did that again, but it would not be my last new idea to entertain the night when he had to check upstairs. His coworker would be there working while he went upstairs.

A few nights later, his coworker did the most unbelievable thing. The room was built under the silo that held the rice. It came down to the point that emptied into a pipe and then transferred to another place. This silo funnel had four compartments in it, and doors on each compartment about two feet across were held in place with four bolts. The plates would be removed each time it was emptied to make sure it was clean and ready for the next batch of rice. There was an old car seat in the room to rest on. That was where I slept each night I stayed. There was a hammer to bang on the metal bin to see if it was empty before removing the door on the silo. It would be apparent it was empty from the sound. For some reason, he unbolted the door and was trying to get them out. The pressure from the rice was pressing on the door, and the bolts would not slide out. He proceeded to drive the bolts out with the hammer. I was asleep on the seat. I usually was at that time.

The banging did not wake me up. I woke up when Dad was pulling the seat with me on it. Had he not showed up when he did, I would have been covered with the rice. Then I saw his coworker was on the rice with his back against the door, trying to keep it from coming out. It would not work because ninety feet of rice still had to come down and out. I heard Dad ask him what he was doing. He said he was checking to make sure it was clean for the next batch to be put in. Dad asked why he did not understand it was full because the door was so hard to open. He just looked at Dad with these sad eyes and shrugged. The place was full of rice, and I would have been buried in it if it were not for Dad. The rest of the night was spent trying to get the rice cleaned up and back in a bin.

Dad had an idea and set the plan in motion. A grain vacuum was a giant vacuum that would suck the rice up and transfer it to another place. The place the trucks dumped their grain was just outside the door. Once it was set up, the work would proceed quickly. By the time the next crew came in, they had it all cleaned up. Clocking out and going home was a good idea after a night like that. I kept thinking about how Dad had saved me from being buried. I knew what death meant. I looked at him all the way home.

When we got home, he told Mom how stupid that was. He did not tell her about how close it was for me. They both were happy about the outcome. I was happy that another night and another close call had ended well. I was still there though. Every kid has close calls all the time. One simple act of forgetting what you are doing—and the whole world comes crashing down. When it does, move the most important things out of danger and then work on the mistake. Use your head and do not panic. Take your time before doing what needs to be done and see if it is the right thing to do. Yes, I also learned from that moment. Listen to the sound that needs to be heard before removing what needs to stay in place.

I will go ahead and tell this short story. The outhouse was the only place to go at the granary. It was beside the road and across from the silos. It had rained the night before, and the ditch was full of water. We had to walk around the ditch to get to the outhouse. If you have never had to use one of these, do not. The holes to sit on were man-sized. I was accustomed to taking off all my clothes to go to the bathroom. I'm not sure why, but it paid off that morning before we went home. Everyone was there for the shift change, and everyone was standing around talking. Dad helped me and stayed with me in the outhouse. As I sat on the hole, I lost my handhold, slipped right through, and fell in—all the way to the bottom. You know where I landed without any other words. I looked up at Dad from the bottom of the hole. I was crying—and rightly so. I'm reasonably sure Dad did not want to touch me. Being naked worked well. The ditches being full of the rain from the night before also helped. Dad said, "Get in the water and wash off." It was cold, but it was so much better than where I had just been. It is not a memory a person wants to remember.

It reminds me of us at times: naked and covered with stink. No one wants to be around us or have anything to do with us. Our only hope is to look up and cry for help. The only thing available is a cold, wet moment, but it is well worth it. When we have fallen so far down, all we can do is look up—and we will do whatever is needed to get clean.

CHAPTER 9

BUBBY MINDING
THE PIGS ON THE ACRE

IT IS NOT always easy to do what was planned from the beginning, but you go ahead and stay with the plan. I still remember the day we got our first pigs. Dad and I went to buy them and bring the pigs home. They were still piglets. They were black with white rings around their shoulders. I did not know what kind they were. I just knew that they were pigs.

Dad had made everything ready for them by fencing off half an acre. I saw him dig down and put the fence underground and asked why he did that. When I was with him and my brother around cattle, I never saw that done. He took the time to tell me about how pigs would root in the ground for food and sometimes root their way under the fence. Once doing so, they would escape and run away. I asked what they ate and why we got two of them. He told me it was so they would have babies, and we could sell them to make money. That sounded good to me. I had so many questions about them, which made me eager to learn all about them. Now they had to have names. Why we named them the names we did, I cannot remember. The male would be called Jodie, and the female would be Nancy.

I found out fast that they would eat anything. Some things were so yucky. Fish heads, table scraps, rice husks, and the like were fed to them daily. Since Dad worked at the granary, we always had lots of rice husks. With the husks also came rats—big monster ugly ones—but that is another story for another time. Jodie and Nancy became pets to me more than anything. I would spend more time with them than with people. I was never afraid of them like most people were. When they were grown, a cousin came over to look at them and told us how to handle them.

I was in the pen with them, doing what I had always done around them. The pigs had gotten big by that time, and Jodie even had tusks sticking out of his mouth. This cousin, Mr. Brave, jumped into the pen with them. He started walking toward them, and they charged at him. Before you could have said jackrabbit, he had run and jumped over the fence in a single bound. My cousin stood there as white as a ghost.

Dad almost laughed his head off. I had left the pigpen while he was there doing his brave act, and I jumped back into the pen to be with them again. Dad just stood there without saying a word. Sure enough, after experiencing my cousin's fear, they charged at me too. The cousin was screaming and carrying on like you would not believe because I was in the pen. A little boy being charged by those two big hogs must have been a sight. Jodie was the first one to reach me. He came full force—right at me. When he got about three feet from me, I doubled up my fist and hit him between the eyes. He stopped on a dime, let out a small grunt, turned, and walked away.

I turned and looked at my cousin and Dad. His face was in total disbelief, and Dad was laughing so hard again. My cousin said he could not believe that that little boy put him to shame for being so scared and running as he did. If a person could really drop their jaw, he did. He started to climb back into the pen. Jodie and Nancy saw him and ran at him again. He never got back in and decided he had something he needed to do. He never came back to give us advice on how to raise hogs.

There came a day when Jodie and Nancy found out they could get out by rooting under the fence. Dad was inside watching wrestling; he always turned the volume full blast when he watched. By then, we had expanded the area for them by another quarter acre. Jodie had found a place the fence was not buried deep enough and began to root under it. I saw what they were doing and grabbed a board to stop them. It did not work. I was screaming at the top of my lungs for help to stop them. No one came, and they got out. I did my best to corner them, but they did not heed me. All I could do was let them run, and they ran down the road toward town. I ran into the house all excited and screaming. Dad and Mom could not understand why I was screaming. When I said the pigs got out, I got action from Dad. Now he had his wrestling match to contend with in real life. Jumping into the car, away we went at the only speed Dad knew in a car: fast!

The hogs had gotten about half a mile down the road. After cornering them and tying a rope around their necks, we got them home. The next thing was repairing the fence. An hour later, it was done. They stood there watching us the whole time. Dad went back to watching television, and I jumped into the pen to spend time with my best friends: Jodie and Nancy.

Another cousin came over another day to look at the hogs. The pen was big, and they had lots of running room. He was not afraid, but he waited for Dad and me to go into the pen with him. He got in and came over to us. The hogs did not pay him any mind, and I was petting them. Suddenly, he picked me up and set me on Jodie. Jodie was not tamed to give rides. I hung on for my life, and halfway across the pen, he bucked me off. Just as soon as I was off his back, he stopped and looked at me. I was not laughing. My cousin was, and Dad had a look of disagreement with what my cousin had done. He did not come back to see the hogs ever again.

On to my imagination while being with them. I had seen Tarzan, and it was my turn to be him. Tall weeds were growing inside the pen, and it looked like a jungle. Some paths had been trodden out by the three of us. I would do the Tarzan shout and walk through tall weeds. The hogs followed me everywhere I went. They were grunting and snorting as they did. I was a real jungle man, and they were my convoy companions. We came upon some hostile natives. I began to fight them and kill them to protect my companions. They had no idea what I was doing. They would just stand there and watch me.

We finally made it back to our camp and put everything away. Since I only had on my shorts for a loincloth, I had little to put away. They were hot by now and went to cool off in their mud spa. I would watch over them all night because of all the dangers that could harm them. I have no idea how many lions, tigers, and panthers I killed to protect them. I do not think they ever gave a thought about how many times I saved them from certain death. The hogs only cared that I was rubbing and petting them. Every day we had some new adventure on the acre.

I noticed Nancy getting fat and told Dad. He said that was why we got them; she was about to have babies. Wow! More pigs to play with. The day came, and she had a lot of little pigs. I watched as they came out and counted them. It seemed natural to me, and I was so happy to see the little ones. For some reason, we did not get to name them. Once the little pigs were weaned from their mom, I found out why we did not name them. Dad sold them. When Dad sold the hogs, it was not a happy day for me. I thought we would have more pigs to play with and raise. I learned some hard facts about the life of animals. While the males were still little, Dad prepared them for becoming dinner for someone later and sold them for that reason. When they were gone, it was just the two of them and me again. By that time, I was in school. One day I got home and ran to see them. Dad and Mom had not said anything. I could not find them in the pen anywhere, and I ran all over the acre looking for them. Then I ran back into the house and told Dad they were gone. That was when he told me they had gotten out again, and he found them on someone's porch. He proceeded to tell me that he loaded them up and sold them to someone to get rid of them. I understood, but I did not understand it at the same time. Why the hurry? Why was I not part of making the decision? I was crushed and went out to where they had been raised and sat for the longest time. I began not to trust going to school. What would be missing the next time I went home?

We did get other pigs to have babies, but I never got close to them like Nancy and Jodie. A lot of pigs were born on the acre, and lots were sold away. Time went by, and one day, I was told we would get another pig. The new piglet looked like Nancy and Jodie. He was all black except for the white ring around his shoulders. It would be my responsibility to raise him. Raising him made me so happy. I was told he would be going to the butcher when he got big enough. I knew what that meant, but I am not sure I did when they told me. I gave him a name, and I named him after myself. Cecil was so gentle, and I fed him good things. Every day, I would tend to whatever he seemed to need. We had adventures together. His pen was not as big as the other ones. He would stand at the fence and watch for me every day. I could tell he was happy when he saw me. He had distinctive grunts and snorts for me. I would run—not walk—to feed him and spent lots of time just talking to him. He was the only one that could understand me at times. He grew and became a big boy.

One morning before sunup, Dad woke me. He said, "Get up and let us go. It is time to do what we have been planning for. It is time to take the hog to the butchers."

I got up and did as I was told.

Dad had the twenty-two rifle in his hand and a knife. Dad had taught me how to shoot the gun, and I had gotten good at hitting the targets. I could shoot the top of a match without damaging the wood. He told me I would have to shoot the hog. Cecil? He placed the gun in my hands and told me where to hold it to his head. Dad told me to keep it steady and pull the trigger. Tears were running down my face, but I did what he told me to. About the time I pulled the trigger, Cecil rooted at the gun, causing me to miss where I was supposed to shoot him. The gun fired and hit him in the leg. He began to run around, squealing as loud as he could. I did not know what to do, and I told Dad I was sorry I had missed. The sound he was making was tearing me apart. I dropped the gun and covered my ears.

Dad jumped into the pen with the knife in his hand, grabbed Cecil's head, and pulled it back until I could see his neck. I saw him take the knife to finish what we came to do. Watching him do this was a frightening sight to see. He was still making sounds—but not for long.

I watched as Dad stood up and asked what had happened. I told him that Cecil bumped the gun about the time I pulled the trigger. This time, he said he wished he had done it, not because of my pain, but because that caused the blood to rush through him and would make the meat not taste as good.

The story is not over yet.

He made me help him load the pig up to take him to the butcher. I would have to watch the butcher put him into this boiling water to remove all his hair. Then stay to watch as they cut him into pieces and wrapped the pieces in white butcher paper packages. Then we loaded him up and took him home where the white packages were put in the freezer. All the others were so happy because we had meat to eat. I never ate one bite of Cecil. During that time only, I became a vegetarian. That was the last pig I ever had anything to do with.

It is not always easy to do what was planned from the beginning, but you go ahead and stay with the plan. Pain is going to happen in life, and sometimes you cannot help it. No matter what you do, you move on and try to be strong—only to return to moments that are memories of days gone by. Be a vegetarian at times.

CHAPTER 10

LEFT ALONE ON THE ACRE—EVERYONE ELSE IN THE HOUSE

Even a child is known by his doings, whether his work be pure, and whether it be right.

—Proverbs 20:11(KJV)

WHY DID THEY not worry? Why did they not wonder what the child was doing? Even a child must be trusted to do what is right at times. You will know if what the child is doing is right if you spend time watching and listening. Was I alone on the acre? I had learned to make the best of things and keep myself busy. Imagination and creativity led me into some fascinating, adventurous—and dangerous times. This section is to let you know what I did to keep myself busy.

Once I was going to dig my way to China. Dad told me that if a person could dig straight through the earth, they would come out in China. That was all it took for me. I believed him and started thinking about how I could do it. The digging tools we had were not always the best. To dig anything with them took lots of force and time to dig even the smallest hole. The ground was smooth at first. I had had no problem removing the husk, dirt-type soil we had on the acre.

For about three inches, I was going to be in China by nightfall or at least before called to supper. It was a dusty job because it was one of those hot summer days. The sun was beating down on my head, but I kept digging. The water hose was nearby to drink from. Just turn the handle and out came all the water I needed. It tasted like the hose, but back then, I did not know any different. Cool water came from the pump Dad had placed for our water to the house and everything else.

I was digging away. With every shovelful tossed aside, dust and dirt came back into my face. No problem there. I would soon be in China and enjoying cooler weather and people I could not understand. As I dug, I thought about how I might be able to talk to them and what I would do with my time there. I had seen pictures at school and thought how pretty everything looked there. I had heard that the people were friendly. I was ready to make friends with some new people.

When I got deeper than three inches, the ground grew hard. I would bang the shovel into the ground; sometimes, it would bounce back at me, shaking my hands and making them tingle. Then I would place my foot on the edge and jump. It was amazing how that helped. I could get half an inch deeper every jump. Jump, bang, jump, bang. I kept at it all afternoon. By suppertime, I had gone about six inches deep. When I went in to eat, Dad asked what I had been doing. They could see from the window that I was digging for some reason. I told him I was digging my way to China. A big smile came across his face, and he said nothing to discourage me.

Early the next morning, I ate my breakfast, which Mom had made for me, and out I went. This time, I just knew I could be there by lunchtime—at least almost there. Drink, dig, drink, dig. Nothing was going to stop me. I was wearing more dirt than I had removed, but I was happy in my shorts and no shirt. That was my wardrobe for summer. Not everyone was dressed as cool as me. Dig, Bubby, dig, I thought. I must be getting closer. One time, I thought I could hear people talking underneath me. I stopped digging to see if I could understand them. They were proving to be sneaky. Every time I stopped digging, they would be quiet also.

I wondered if the people were going to be as friendly as I had thought. Never mind if they are or are not—it will be okay. I have to get there. Another four inches.

"Come and eat, Bubby."

Oh no, I will never get this done if they do not stop calling me to eat.

Mom said, "What are you digging for out there, Bubby?"

"I am going to China."

Everybody smiled. Their smiles, to me, were a sign of approval. Little did I know it was not for that. Dinner was over. Where I grew up, breakfast came first, then dinner, and then supper. (I think Bubby is still trying to figure out this eating schedule.)

I went back out and began to dig. The ground grew a little softer. Instead of half an inch, I could dig an inch with each shovelful. I knew I would make it. The softer ground must mean I am getting close to digging all the way through.

The voices had stopped. It must have been because they knew I would be popping out of the ground at any moment. I was at least two feet deep now, and my little body was about halfway down. The sun was hot during that time of day. A weeping willow provided shade for a while. Those trees weep all the time on you. It was time to dig again. Are you getting as tired as I was back then? I agree with you—and so did Bubby. He finally gave up on his quest to get to China. By the time I had stopped, I had a three-foot-deep and three-foot-wide hole. We will not end the story of the hole.

For the next few days, I would go out and sit in the hole. It was cooler, and I could put something over it, which made it even more refreshing. One time, I went to sleep while I was sitting there. Mom found me, woke me up, and told me not to do that again.

Since I could not get to China, I had to think of something else to do with the hole. It did not take long. My mind must have been missing the soldiers I lost in the fire. They reappeared in my mind, and we were off to war again. The hole became headquarters and the foxhole to hide in. I had the ideal army this time. No one could see them but me. The opposing army did not have a chance to win. The battles would be furious. Some of my men would die from grenade explosions or gunshots, but it was okay because I could bring them back to life by thinking them alive. The battle lasted for about a week. As the leader of my army, I knew they needed rest and reinforcements.

I had a friend who would come over to visit sometimes. Yes! He was real. We were about the same age. He got right to work with my imaginary war and joined forces with me. Calling back and forth on makeshift walkie-talkies, we would tell our men where to go. The hole was getting small with so many people. We moved our headquarters to the mountain, and we could see the enemy coming from all directions. We were unstoppable. We never lost a battle. By the end of three weeks (suppertime), we had declared victory. It was time for him to take his men home.

Dad did not fill up the hole. I was able to have it for many adventures during the next few weeks. It was my road to China that never went away. I still think of the people there and wonder how it would feel to meet them in their own country.

That was not all I did by myself. Here is the most magnificent adventure. I got the idea to build a clubhouse. It was to be the biggest clubhouse ever. This time, I needed help. I asked Dad about building it. I never thought he would not help, but he did. We went right to work. We had some old lumber and sheets of tin lying around. The nails were rusty, and some were bent. Dad had already shown me how to use a bent nail. He helped me put four posts in the ground to fasten the walls to. Digging again? This time, the holes would be smaller and not so deep. They only needed to hold the posts until we had the walls in place.

At first, it would not have a door, but in my mind, no one could see in. With a dirt floor and gaps in the planks, it was coming along nicely. It took a few days to complete. I would keep working on it—even when Dad could not help me. (Today, we would call it a man cave.) I felt like the luckiest boy ever. When any friends came over, they would talk about how they wished they could have one. Since they could not, I had friends come over more often. We would sit in the clubhouse and talk about everything. Dad and Mom never seemed to check on me. I was on the acre; what could I possibly get into that was dangerous? The clubhouse was included in many discussions in the days to follow. I thought about what I could do and who I could invite to come spend time with me. I did think about inviting the president a couple of times. Sister would play games with me, and Little Sister would come out when Mom would let her.

It stood just about in the middle of the acre. I could see all around it. When it rained, I could still play inside. Because the roof was made of tin, it did not leak. The floor never got muddy. My furniture was so comfortable. All of it was just like what I wanted. I had one little wooden chair. It had arms and armrests with a height that was right for my age. I would let others sit on it, but not for long. The clubhouse lasted for a few years and gave me joy every day. Having a place to go was so special. No one ever asked what I was doing when I went to the clubhouse. Privacy and contentment—what more could a little boy want?

Neighbors moved in next door. Dad had not built a fence between the properties, but he did plant hedges part of the way. The new neighbors had two kids—a boy who was older than me and a younger girl. The man was a mechanic and a welder. His son and I did not get along too well, but we still played together. I got along with his sister better. We were closer in age. They would walk to school with Sister and me. I was not sure he liked his sister playing with me. He would interrupt our playtime.

The man would offer to help work on our cars without asking for money in return. His wife was also friendly to us. They lived there for a few years. One day, the girl did not come over to play. I was not sure, but it seemed like they did not like something that happened from the day before, and she had to stay home. It must have gotten settled because she was back the day after.

Many times, Dad and I would witness things wherever we would go. When it did not seem right, I would look at my dad, and he would look at me. We would turn around and walk away from what we had seen. As soon as we would get home, he spent time talking about the event and helped me understand what was wrong or right with the event we had seen. My dad helped me understand that sometimes people do things for a reason, and we should be patient until we know the full outcome of the event.

Now there was no fence, but with these new neighbors, it would have been easy and tempting to leave the acre. The boy had a bike and would ride it around their yard. He brought it over one day. I tried to ride it, but I was unsuccessful. Now, having no fence made it hard to stay on the acre. There seemed to be an invisible marker between the acres. I would be running and playing when I would realize I needed to stop. Every time I did, I would be right at the edge of the acre before stepping across the line. This invisible fence went all the way around the acre. Mysteries of the acre holding us on it were not really mysteries. It was merely obeying Mom and Dad about not leaving the acre. The neighbor kids tried over and over to get my sister and me to come across the line. We never did unless Dad or Mom were with us.

I was amazed when I watched the neighbor welding. A bright light like lightning would come from his handheld torch. It was the electro touching the metal and melting it. I was told never to look at the light without something on my eyes to protect them. I did notice he had a helmet with a darkened glass to protect his eyes. The welding rod would smoke and make sounds of burning like lightning hitting it. When he was done, he would hit it with this strange hammer, and a flaky thing would pop off where he had welded. They called it slag; it was impurities in the metal that would settle to the top of the weld. I wanted to try it, but I was not given a chance. He did weld things for us, and we got used to having things welded for us for free. When they moved away, we lost that help. A few years later, Dad bought a welder, and I learned to use it. By high school, I was able to win fourth place in the state competition. Maybe there will be more about that in the next book.

We also had neighbors move in on the other side of the acre during that time. They also had kids who would come over to play. The girl was in my class since I had been held back in first grade. The first girl and the new neighbor girl formed a friendship, and we played together all the time. Unlike the first neighbors, these neighbors would let her stay and play when they needed to do something. It was fun having these new friends come over.

We had many adventures together. We were not into boy and girl relationships. We were all still young enough just to have fun. There was no jealousy between us, but sometimes they wanted to be girls. I would find something else to do during those times. It would not be long until they would come and want to join me. The three of us did a lot together on the acre. After the first one's family moved away, the second one also moved away. Well, it happened again. I lost my friends. The first girl moved back later in life, but we did not have the same friendship. The other girl was a friend at school until we graduated.

I went back to playing by myself except when a friend from school could come and play, which was not too often. The cousins would sometimes come for a few hours. The acre was my friend that did not leave me.

One corner of the acre became the curiosity corner. Dad and I would walk out to the corner and step across the road to the landing field for the planes. We would sometimes just stand and watch them come down the field and lift off into the air. Vroom! They would fly by, and the pilot would wave. When he came back to land, he would load more fertilizer to spray the crops in the area. From the corner of the acre, Dad would let me walk with him up the fencerow that separated the fields. Walking up the fencerow to see the planes did make it tempting to leave the acre by myself. I wanted to walk up there by myself in the worst way. I would run out to the corner and look as far as I could see at times.

Across the road to the north, there was a farm where the owner had pecan trees. Every year after harvest time, the owner would tell Dad that we could pick up what was left. They were so good, and it was lots of fun breaking them open to eat the goodies that came from the inside. I was so tempted to cross the road to pick them up, mainly before they harvested them. There were so many just lying there. Dad made sure he told me about being honest, and it was not right to pick them up unless we had permission. My sister and I never crossed the road to pick them up until we were told to do so.

Sometimes Dad, Sister, and I would walk up to the fencerow. We found a plant called poke salad that was growing wild. We would pick it and take it home. Mom would cook it with eggs and bake some cornbread, and that would be our supper. The plant was very poisonous, but since Mom knew how to cook it, it would not hurt us. I would still enjoy a pot of it today, truth be told.

Something else grew up the fencerow, and Dad called them muscadines. They grew on a wild vine and looked like grapes. They tasted good, but there were not many growing at the same time—just enough to cause a small boy to want to sneak off the acre to get some. They would be the wild berries that danced for me in my dreams until Dad took me for a fencerow walk again.

One day, two of my uncles came over to talk to Dad. They were talking about the fencerow and buried treasure. Now, that had my ears perking up. Dad had a steel rod in his hand. He, my uncles, and I began to walk up the other side of the fencerow. We walked about half a mile until we came to where another fence joined it from across the field. The area was grown over with weeds, bushes, and trees. They talked about these bank robbers who had buried their loot in that spot. They talked about how much it was and how they could use the money.

Dad had also brought a hammer with the rod. The three of them placed the steel rod and began to drive it into the ground. Dad was hammering when it sounded like he hit something. He told them it was the radiator from their car that they used to cover and protect the money. Then he hit it again, and it went deeper. Then he said, "Did you hear that? It sounds like gold?"

Little Bubby was thinking, Why didn't they bring a shovel?

They talked more and then decided to leave. They talked about other buried treasure they knew about as they walked home.

After my uncles left, I asked Dad when we were going to go back to dig up the money. He smiled and said, "Someday."

That was when I decided that Dad was joking with his brothers. There was no buried treasure. All those stories were fabricated to keep older people entertained. Bubby was not as naive as some people thought. He would let people have their dreams too. I did enjoy those stories, but it was mostly because I got to get off the acre with Dad.

It is getting late in the day, and I have been talking for days. I think I might go and eat those leftovers Mom left on the stove all day and called it a day. Yep! That is what I am going to do. Time to watch Bonanza all cuddled up next to Dad. Hoss loves his brothers. Little Joe needs to stop getting into so much trouble. I wonder what Adam will do when he leaves the ranch. Ben would call the boys together, and Hop Sing would feed them. Maybe time for Rifleman too. Off to bed now for all of us. Good night, everyone.

CHAPTER 11

GOING TO WORK
WITH DAD

HOW PEOPLE TREAT children will influence them forever. It could be useful sometimes—or it could be harmful. Be careful with every moment you are with them; they are watching and learning. Please let me clarify that this is one of those "no judgment chapters in our lives." You will soon know why I said what I just said.

Even before the fire, Dad would take me to work with him. He and Mom thought I would be safer with him than in the cotton fields where I could put cotton in my mouth that had been poisoned for bugs. I was so happy to always go with Dad. His love for me and mine for him could not be matched. He was Babe, and I was Dad, which was our agreement from when I was four years old. He worked at the granary during harvest season. There were silos, bins, and buildings to store grain in. A lot of equipment was set around. The railroad stretched the length of the grain yard. All kinds of Trucks would bring their grain in from the farm.

While there, I was glued to Dad's leg most of the time. I am sure it looked like he had a growth on his leg. To get his attention, I would poke him with what he called "the boniest finger ever made." When I poked him with my finger, he would jump every time. It was like a needle, he said. He would always look down and ask what I needed. If he did not, I kept poking, poking, and poking. There were lots of things that I could have gotten into. I knew the best and safest place was right by Dad (Babe).

The farmers' wives would sometimes be with their husbands, and while they were waiting to unload their grain, the wives would walk into town. It was not too long a walk, and they could pick up things they needed. The farmers' wives would see me and think I was the cutest little guy. They would talk to me and try to get me to walk over to them. I would always look up at Dad to get his permission. Once I had his permission, I would walk over to them and talk until their husbands had unloaded their grain. I was happy to do this because they would walk away from the dusty area. I also enjoyed getting special attention.

After a few trips, the women would come looking for me as soon as they got there. Some would even have treats. One day, one of them wanted to know if I could walk to town with her and go to the store. I looked at Dad, and he gave his permission. The walk to the store was so much fun, and I was so excited. She got me a few things, and we headed back to the granary. On the way back, I became too tired to walk. She had to carry me back while carrying the other things she had bought. I did feel sorry for her, but I just could not walk anymore. It was hot, and my little legs could not make it back.

When we got back to where Dad was, she told Dad what had happened. He felt terrible also. I did not get to walk to town very many times after that. Dad would tell the women what might happen. If I did go, there was an agreement about walking the whole way. If I did get tired, we would stop and rest and then go again. Taking that much time lets you know how long it took to unload the trucks.

The events of this chapter occurred before the fire. My brothers were still alive and watching over me all the time. When they were not helping Mom pick cotton, they would ride into town and stay for the day. They would find all kinds of exciting things to do at the place where Dad worked. The grain was stored in flat silos that were about fifty feet across. The way the rice was stored in them caused the rice to create a long slope to the floor if the bin was not full. The silo was divided into sections with wood walls, and different types of rice were stored in each one. To get to each bin, a person would have to climb up the ladder that was attached to the silo and climb onto the metal mesh catwalk. With no rice in them, it was about fifteen feet down to the concrete floor. If there was rice in the sections, there was not much fear of falling and getting hurt. One day, my brothers took me into one of these silos. They also brought a scoop shovel. A scoop shovel is a big shovel that moves grain in larger volumes with one scoop at a time.

My brothers took me with them, and I am not sure what Dad was doing to let them take me. They helped me onto the walkway and guided me down to the place they were going. It was a bin that was about halfway full. Rice was placed in the bins so that one side was at the top of the bin, and on the other side of the bin, the rice was down to the concrete. They set me on the walkway and told me to stay. They climbed down onto the rice and waded up the rice to the top with the shovel. Then I saw them do the most fantastic thing.

I had never seen snow sledding or anything like it. My brothers took the handle of the shovel and held it out in front of them. Then they would sled down the rice like it was snow. Whoosh! Down they would come like a snow shield, except faster. Each of them would take a turn. I watched them slide down the rice for the longest time. They were having so much fun.

My brothers were always having fun, and they would include me too. Sliding down on the shovel was too dangerous for little Bubby, but I did not mind that I did not get to slide. There are some things I would not attempt to do. To this day, I have held to this belief. I was so excited about watching them. One at a time, and then they had to try two, which was not a good idea. The younger brother was the best at it. He seemed to have it down to an art. I can see them now and the joy on their faces. They were laughing so hard at each other. Rice could be as dangerous as quicksand at times. You had to know how to walk on it. It ran like water at times and pressed hard on everything it came to rest on.

The four of us spent an hour or so there and then came out of the silo. My brothers helped me climb down the ladder to safety. I stayed with them until we got to Dad. There was still lots of time before Dad got off work. They went to town, and I got to go with them. My older brother carried me most of the way without me asking him to. They walked all over town and went from store to store, and there were not many: a store for food, another for clothes and food, and the drug store for ice-cream cones. It was so yummy and so cold, which was just what I was ready for.

The next trip into town, when Dad would be working, was on Saturday. I remember that trip so well. My brothers took me to see a cowboy movie.

Popcorn and drinks were part of the adventure. Look at those big horses on the big screen. That cowboy is ten feet tall. I was poking and poking my older brother with my bony little finger. "Look, look, did you see that?"

He would simply look at me and smile. "Yes, I saw that—now keep watching."

Now that I look back, I think he had more fun watching me than he did watching the movie. The theater was full. Kids were screaming and yelling about what was happening on the big screen. That was the most significant moment my brothers gave me for that day. There were many days that all of them, in their way, would make me happy.

My middle brother would put airplane models together and hang them from the ceiling. He had so many, and it was hard for me to see the ceiling at times. He was always putting one together. When he could not hang any more planes, he had to do something with some of them. I got excited every time he needed to because he gave them to me.

I got a little sidetracked there. I was talking about going to work with Dad. Dad would have to go into the silos to get them ready for the grain that would be stored there. The buildings were bigger than gymnasiums. He would have to sweep them and prepare the floor for long metal things that had small holes in them. They would then be connected to fans that were outside. The fans would pull air through the rice and ventilate the rice. Without this method, the rice would mold. He taught me all about them and how they worked. Helping Dad is where I learned so much about sweeping and putting small screws into things like an erector set. He would tighten each one I put in.

Not many tools were needed. A strong back and steady hands made for excellent working conditions. These ventilator ducks were about six feet apart and ran the width of the building. I saw the importance of them one time when the rice was removed. There were spots that ventilation had not worked, and the rice was black and stuck together. What a terrible odor too! The work was not done until the mold, dust, and stink were all cleaned up. I learned that you had to wear a mask; otherwise, the mold and dust could kill you. It became a part of everyday life, learning what can kill you and how to keep it from doing so. He taught me that the floors had to be clean and how to sweep them without making lots of dust. I learned fast because I could not stand all that dust in the air. Child labor—or a boy and his father sharing moments of a lifetime?

He didn't let me go upstairs to the top of the tall silos until I was a teenager. He would leave me downstairs by myself. When he worked nights, I got so interested in the train that came by about midnight. I would stand out there and wave at the engineer every night. He would always wave back and give me a big smile. This went on for weeks. When Dad was not downstairs, I would go out and wave at the engineer. It was the most beautiful train, and it was so long. It would take forever to pass by. Car after car was hooked on for them to be pulled. He never forgot me and was ready to wave. Week after week, we would wave back and forth.

One night, as I was standing there, the train stopped. I was not sure what to do. I stood there and watched it stop entirely. The engineer climbed out of the engine room, walked over to me, introduced himself, and asked where my father was.

I led him into the grain elevator office where Dad was. I went over to Dad and said, "This is him."

Dad looked at him, and I am sure he was wondering what I had done to this man I had brought to see him.

The engineer introduced himself to Dad and the other worker, and then he told Dad that he was taken with me standing out there every night to wave at him. Dad thanked him for coming in. He then asked Dad if he could take me onto the train. Dad agreed and went with us.

To my great surprise, he began to tell me what each handle did. He said, "I want you to know what they do. I am going to let you pull and push them to get the train going."

Dad stood there and watched with eyes as open as mine. This little boy was about to cause tons and tons of metal and goods to move down the track. He pointed to each handle that I needed to use, and I heard the engine speeding up. The train began to move down the track. In all your imagination, you would never guess how excited I was. I had never imagined getting to do something like that. The train moved slowly, and in about a hundred yards, he told me to pull this handle, and when I did, the train began to slow down.

He told me to push another handle, and the train stopped. I looked at him, and he looked at me—and then we both looked at Dad. The ride of a lifetime was over.

"Not so fast, you two. He must back this train up to where we got on," he said.

Backing up a train is not easy, and the whistle must be blown.

"Here you are, young man," he said as he lifted me. "Pull on this cord right here."

When I did, the whistle was so loud. It was around midnight.

"Do it again. The people must know we are coming back." He stood me up on the floor, and he told me which handles to pull and push. Backward we went.

Dad was as surprised as I was.

When we got almost back to where we started, he told me what to do. We climbed out of the engine, and I looked back up at the monster I had just moved. I did not notice that he and Dad talked a long time while I looked at the train. He and Dad exchanged information about where each other lived. He and Dad became friends that night, and he would stop many times to talk with Dad and me. As a teenager, Dad asked if I remembered him. I most certainly did. He had become someone I looked up to that night. Dad told me he had died that week. A drunk driver had hit him and killed him. I stayed sad for days.

A few days after the train trip, I decided I needed engineer boots.

Dad said no and went to work upstairs. When he got back, I asked why I could not get them. He looked down and pointed at my shoes. They were not too old. He told me that when I wore them out, I might get the boots. He left again and came back after some time had gone by. I thought about what he said and was not sure how long it would take to wear them out. I could walk around all night—maybe that would work. A little dirt all over them might also help. When he got back, I asked what he meant about wearing them out. He told me that when the soles came off, they would be worn out. He said he would be back in a little bit, and he had to check the level of the rice. The next room was a tool shop. I needed the boots. I did not just want them.

I put my shoes in the vise and turned the handle until it was tight on the shoe. I took hold of the hammer and something to pull with. They must have been almost worn out anyway. The soles just popped right off.

In no time, my shoes were worn out completely. It took Dad longer to come back than normal. I was so eager to show him that my shoes were worn out.

When he got back, I was holding my shoes up to show him they were worn out. He did not get mad, but he should have. He took the blame for me doing it and said, "I should have seen this coming. Now, what will we do?"

I had to wear worn-out shoes for the rest of the night. Before going home the next morning, we made a fast trip into town. I went home with engineer boots. I did feel bad—but not bad enough to not wear my boots. I would wear those shoes all the time. During the summer, I never wore shoes. Later in life—once I was on my own and married—I did buy the train set.

It was family time at work with Dad. I had an uncle who also worked there. One day, the three of us were back in the bins to get them ready for the grain. We were sweeping and putting the air vents together. Dad had to get some things to finish the job, and he left me with my uncle.

My uncle asked me if I wanted to learn some new words about work. "Yes," I said.

He picked up the broom and said, "This is a broom."

I knew that—even at this age.

He said, "But you can call it by a different name." He called it a bad word.

I said the word, and he laughed so hard. I must have said it right, I thought.

He called the wrench in my hand another bad word. He also told me that work was called a bad word. I had learned my new vocabulary, and he told me not to tell Dad what I had learned.

Dad came back, and we finished the work. I did not tell Dad or use any of the words—just like my uncle said. We were standing around because it was about quitting time. My uncle's wife came to pick him up after work. I stood there by Dad as my uncle got into the driver's seat. I pulled loose from Dad, and I ran to the passenger side of the car. The window was down, and I said I needed to tell my aunt something. Dad was standing right by me, and I told her that my uncle and I had been working—but I called it the bad word!

She had a look of horror on her face. "A word like that coming out of such a little mouth?"

I explained that my uncle had taught me the word.

She turned and gave him a look that should have killed him.

He put the car in gear and spun rocks everywhere as he tried to get out of there.

Dad had heard it all, and his looks were about the same. He grabbed me just in time to keep me from getting hurt from the flying rocks and the car fishtailing. The motor was almost screaming; it was so loud.

I looked at my dad and asked what I had done. He took me aside from everyone. Everyone had heard and seen what happened. He got down where he could look me in the face and asked what else I had learned. I told him my uncle told me not to tell. He used my name this time. "Bubby, I need to know what he told you."

He was pale by the time I had finished all my new vocabulary. He told me that those were terrible and naughty words and not to use them again. I felt so bad that I had used them when talking to my aunt. I also felt so bad because I did not know any better.

I was never left alone with him again. I think Dad had some choice words of his own with him the next day. Dad would always laugh when he remembered how my aunt looked when I told her that my uncle taught them to me. He even told me that was the best part, but it was still wrong. Years later, Dad would still laugh about it—and then he would tell me why he was laughing. I listened to Dad, and I never used those words again. My uncle would still use them around me when Dad was not there. When I became a teenager, I got him to stop using those words when he was around me.

On another day, Dad had to clean an area up that had been used as a dumping area for unwanted things. Old broken boards, paint cans, oil cans, and pieces of metal needed to be loaded up and hauled away. I was helping him put all I could on the truck. I would try to pick up things that were way too heavy for me. I thought I could do what he was doing. I would try anything that Dad did. My little hands were too small to handle some of it, and he would tell me to let it go and that he would pick it up.

We had most of it picked up when we came to some empty oil cans. I thought I could them. He helped me get them on the truck, but then he found one that was unopened and full. He talked for a minute with me and told me it was free game since it was in a pile. He put it in the back of our car and then went back to load the rest of the junk. We had almost finished when he dropped what he had in his hand. He looked at me and then walked to the car. I saw him take the can of oil and head toward the buildings where that kind of stuff was stored. I walked with him and asked what he was doing.

He said, "I am going to put it back on the shelf."

I said, "I thought you said it was free game since someone threw it away?"

He said, "I did say that, but I was wrong. Just because someone else did something wrong does not make it right for me to do something wrong. It would belong to the company even if it were thrown away. We need to take care of things that belong to others as well as our own."

After placing it on the shelf with all the other oil, we went back to doing what we were doing before. He talked more about what he had done. He explained so much that morning about being honest in everything we do. "What seems right to one person does not make it right. There are rights and wrongs in the world. Taking care of people and the things that belong to them will be better in the end than if we do not care enough to do so."

I listened to every word that came from him that morning. I think I wrote it on my heart like it was written in stone.

As you can tell, he made a big impression on me that morning, and that has been a part of who I have become ever since. I was a young child, but I could be impressed to do many things. He was always gentle and explained things to me in a manner that I could understand. Most of the time, he made sure I walked right beside him—never behind and never in front. Most of the time, he treated me like an adult. He helped me by lifting me to his level. Honesty is the best policy, and I learned it that day from the one who mattered most in my life. Thanks, Dad, for all you did over all the years of my life.

CHAPTER 12

THE TIME I SCARED
DAD AT WORK

CHILDREN CAN GET into things that will make you wonder how they did what they did. You may not want to know. Do not ask if you do not want the answer. Once you know, it may scare the living daylights out of you.

There were many times I scared Mom and Dad. It just happens when children are growing up. This part of my story is about when Mom was not there because I had gone to Dad's work with him. There were always dangers where Dad worked. A person did not have to look for it; it was there waiting for anyone who came along. Before the man-lift was installed, the workers had to climb a ladder that was connected to the side of the silo to get upstairs. To get to the top, people had to climb rungs on the side of the silo. The steel rods were bent to make a ladder that was placed in the concrete silo. The person climbing the ladder had to pay attention to what they were doing and be ready to climb ninety feet above the concrete floor. They were not easy to hang onto. Sometimes they would have dust on them, which made them slippery.

One night, Dad was almost to the top when his feet and hand slipped. He hung on to the one rung with one hand until he could get his footing again. When he came back down, he was shaking. He did not go back up until he had regained his courage and strength. It had almost pulled his shoulder out of place. The pain in his shoulder lasted for days.

A few months later, a coworker was climbing the same ladder and slipped. He was not able to hang on and fell about sixty feet. He lived, but he was never the same. His entire demeanor changed, and he even lost his family. It took months for the company to install the man-lift that would lift people to the top.

The outside silos contained dangers of their own. Those were the silos my brothers had taken me into. They were shaped like a silo on its side. To enter them, a person had to climb a metal ladder that was bolted to the side of the end wall. After climbing about fifteen feet, a person would have to work around objects that could be a danger and then climb up to the walkway that reached down the center of the silo.

The walkway was built of metal mesh and iron that hung from pipes on the ceiling of the silo. It was only eighteen inches wide. There were no banners or handholds along the full length of the walkway. It also hung close to the ceiling, and you would have to bend over to walk down it if you were more than five feet tall. The silo was divided into sections by walls that were built from lumber planks. Each wall was connected to the next with a steel cable for support. Once a section was full of rice, the wall could give way to the empty bin and collapse into the empty one. To stop this from happening, each section would be filled to counterbalance the one next to it.

The sections had to be maintained all the time. The rice was like water and would flow where it wanted to go. To remove the grain from the bins in the silo, men would have to connect a grain vacuum outside to the pipe leading inside and vacuum out the grain. Dad and another worker were given this task all the time. One time, I got to go with them into the silo to watch them vacuum out the grain.

Dad helped me to the walkway and guided me to where their work would be. The sections were not dangerous if they were all full of rice. If a person fell off the walkway, the rice was a soft place to land. Without rice in the bin, it was more than fifteen feet down to the concrete floor. Dad sat me on the wall of one of the sections and told me to stay there and watch them work. I did what he told me to. If I could see him, all was well.

They connected the pipes leading outside and proceeded to vacuum out the rice. The section began to empty down to a corner near the next section over from me. They were close to the wall, and the noise of the vacuum was loud. I saw the wall next to them begin to fall over onto them. I screamed my heart out and tried to warn them. They looked up at the wall coming toward them, and they did their best to run up the rice hill. However, the rice moved from under their feet, and they could not get out of the way. There was nothing I could do except watch my dad and his coworker get trapped by the rice and wall that was falling on them. I screamed more and cried out for help, but no help would come. No one was listening. I remember the fear I had at that time; I distinctly knew what was about to happen. I was losing my dad. I did not turn to look away like I did during the fire. I watched it until it was all over.

With the noise of the vacuum still going and them doing their best to get out, things were not looking suitable for the end of this story. I noticed the cable attached from section to section doing what it was meant to do. On the side where they were, it got loose. On the other side, it got tight. It held the wall enough to keep the wall from falling over. When I saw this, I hoped they would make it. They never gave up trying to climb out of the rice.

Once they made it to where I was, I grabbed my dad and hung onto him so tightly. If I had been any older, I would have squeezed his breath out of him. They were both breathing hard, and the look on their faces was one of relief. They had just escaped death. They finished getting the rice out, and they removed the rice from each section down to an equal level of each section, which caused each wall to have the same pressure from each side. These were lessons to learn amid dangerous moments. Remove the danger by making all things equal. By the end of the day, they had emptied all the sections they were sent to do.

Never enough excitement for me, right?

The grain had been loaded onto train cars that would carry it to a processing plant where it would be made ready to eat. The boxcars would also have to be prepared, but that is another thing to be talked about another time.

I had been scared enough while watching Dad do his work. Now it was my turn to scare him—but not on purpose. A little preparation for this part may be needed. I had been in the silos many times. The first time up, he allowed me to climb the iron ladder on my own. Dad was right there with his arms around me to catch me if I fell. There was a piece of jagged metal sticking out that the men had not seen, but it caught me. It cut through my shirt and cut my side. I began to bleed a lot, and I cried out.

Dad got me down as fast as he could and went into the office for bandages. A few of the guys gathered around to watch. It took a little time for the bleeding to stop and for me to stop crying. The metal had cut through my shirt and my skin, but it was not deep enough for stitches.

Once I stopped bleeding, and the scare was over, we went back to the ladder. Dad took a hammer and fixed the jagged piece of iron. I went back up and climbed on my own to get to the top of the wall. The walkway was unreachable for me. Dad would have to help me get on the walkway every time he took me into the silo.

He took me with him many times, and he always helped me get on the walkway. He would keep his hand on me because there were no banners or railings to hold onto. After he finished the job, he would bring me out and go back for the tools.

There was one time that he did not let me go with him. I am not sure why he did not, but I remember that he was out of my sight. No one was watching over me, and I was free to do whatever I wanted.

Out of sight did not mean "out of mind" for me. I knew where Dad was and how I could get to him, but there was the problem of getting onto the walkway. I could not reach anything the grown men could to pull myself up and get on the walkway. Before climbing up the iron ladder, I thought long and hard about how to do it. Once I was at the top of the wall, the sections of bins were all empty, meaning there was nothing but concrete floor to land on if I fell. If a man fell, he might break a leg since it was only fifteen feet down to the concrete. I got to the top of the ladder and was looking around at my possibilities. I needed to get to the walkway. I sat there for a little while and looked at all my possibilities. I had been away from Dad for too long by that time.

Looking around, I saw these two-by-fours nailed flat in a Z shape on the inside of the wall that went up to the walkway. I had to think of a way how to reach them. It was over the empty section of the silo. I had to balance myself on the wall, which was six inches wide, over to the Z. I would grip the two-by-fours with the ends of my fingers until I could place the end of my shoes on them. I slowly worked my way to where I was clinging to the wall by holding onto the two-by-fours. A picture of these two-by-fours would leave no doubt about what I am saying.

I worked up to the walkway and climbed on. No one knew what I was doing or where I was. Everyone probably thought I was already with Dad, and he thought others were watching me. Once I was on the walkway, I went back down to the wall and then back up. After doing this a few times, nothing was too hard to do. I did not pay any attention to the floor below.

I was ready to walk down the walkway to my dad. It was dusty, and the air was hard to see through. I could make out his image down at the other end, and I began my journey toward him. At first, he thought I was one of the other workers. When he saw it was me, he tried to stay calm. I heard his voice telling me to stop and not move. He walked toward me, all bent over, and I was able to stand upright and almost run to him.

This time, he screamed, which he hardly ever did. "Stop! Do not move. Let me come to you."

I finally stopped and waited for him.

When he got to me, he was breathing so heavily. I could not think of any reason for him to be like that.

He took me by my hand and led me back to where he had been. He had a rope for some reason—I think to let his tools down to the floor where he was working—and he used the rope to let me down. He climbed down a wooden ladder that had been nailed parallel to the wall of the section. When we got down, he hugged me for the longest time. He asked me why I did that, and I thought, Did what? I got what he was talking about and told him I was missing him because he had been gone for a long time. He hugged me again and told me he was sorry. I was looking around at what he was doing and saw the tools on the floor. I wanted to help. He needed some other tools and told me to stay because he thought I could not get out. The rungs on the wooden ladder were too far apart for me to use. When he climbed out and went for the tools, I was left alone in that bin. I heard noises, and it was not Dad. It was the first time I had been left in a place like that by myself.

I played with the tools a little while. Dad was not back yet, and I needed to find him again. If the Z worked for me, the two-by-fours on this ladder would too. I gripped the two-by-four with my fingers as I had done earlier. I held it until I could reach the next rung, and then I would pull myself up until my feet were on the rung. It was not long before I was at the top of the wall. I walked the wall over to the walkway and climbed up on it. I was on my way out when I saw Dad coming.

"Stop!" he shouted again. His eyes were so wide. He looked down into the bin and said, "How did you …" He let me back down to the floor with the rope, and then he went down to collect all the tools. He turned to me and said, "How did you get up on the walkway by yourself?"

I went over to the ladder, and before he could get close enough, I had scaled the wall again. By then, he was gasping for air.

I waited for him on the walkway.

He came up out of the bin and gathered everything up, and we headed down the walkway toward the entrance. We stopped, and he looked everything over. Dad looked at me and then back at the great expanse between the walkway and the outside ladder. He asked me how I had gotten from that spot to the walkway.

I said, "Just like this." Before he knew it, I was on the two-by-fours, making my way back down to the wall and onto the edge of the wall and heading for the ladder. Had there been a pin dropped from the far end of that building, you could have heard it hit the concrete below. He did not say a word. Later, he told me it was best to not try to help me. It was all he could do to stop himself. If he had, we both would have fallen most likely. Once we were on the ground outside, he looked a little pale. I was so happy and proud of what I had done to get to him. He was relieved that we had made it out alive. An event like that never happened again—there.

I have one more true story for this section. The next year, I was still allowed to go to work with Dad at night. The same person who he always worked with was there. I spent a lot of time talking with this person and liked him. Dad had gone up to check the flow of the rice, and I was left alone in the little silo office. There was a workbench across one side where they could fill out reports and keep documents. A stool was next to the bench so that people could do paperwork. Dad and his coworker had gone out. I was sleepy, but I did not want to admit it. As I sat on the stool, I let my head down and fell asleep on the bench. I was out of it and sleeping so well. Dad's coworker saw me asleep and thought it would be funny to scare me by jumping into the room and screaming. Dad's coworker had once caused all the trouble by letting the rice get loose in that silo office.

As I slept, the coworker jumped into the room, causing the door to bang against the wall. He screamed at the top of his lungs, and I jumped off the stool and out of my skin. I am sure my eyes looked like saucers by then. You did not have to look for the whites of my eyes, and they were all you could see in the room. My heart was racing, and I could feel it trying to beat out of my chest. I was trying to catch my breath. He was laughing so hard that he lost his breath. I was standing there, but I did not say a word. I gave him a look of disgust. He would not stop his uncontrollable laughing.

Dad walked in and was wondering what he was laughing so hard at. He replayed the whole show for Dad to hear. Dad did not laugh, and he said, "I do not think you should have done that."

The coworker looked at Dad and asked, "Why not? The little guy cannot do anything about it—and it was so funny."

Dad said, "I do not think that you should have done that."

The coworker went about his work, still laughing, and Dad made sure I was okay. He reassured me that everything was okay.

I thought that it was okay too.

Dad's coworker came in and laughed more and retold what I looked like. It was time for revenge—the kind that makes people regret what they have done to others. Dad came and checked on me, and I told him it was going to be okay. Dad was not sure what I meant, but he knew something was about to happen.

It was about midnight, and it was dark except for some dim lights. I stood in a shadow at the end of one building where I knew Dad's coworker had to pass. I stood in the shadow—enough that he would not see me until he passed by—but he could feel me looking at him. I never said a word. He noticed me as I had hoped for, snickered, and said, "Okay, you got me." Then he went on his way.

About an hour later, I placed myself in another spot like that one. He came by and did not see me in the shadow until it was too late. He jumped back and screamed a little. Now he did not think that what he did was funny anymore. I let another hour go by and knew it was time for him to do something at another place. I did not scare him this time because he was looking for me. He laughed and told me I did not get him.

The whole time, I never said a word. He told Dad what I had done. Dad looked at me and smiled. I was good with Dad when I saw him smile.

Let the night continue, I thought. One more time, I hid in the shadows before he came by. He was caught off guard. There were words this time, and he kept on walking. By the time he got to the next area, I was waiting. He had not expected that. No shadow seemed to be without me. Wherever he went, I was there waiting.

It was about an hour and a half before their shift was over. Dad's coworker was talking with Dad about what I was doing to him.

Dad said, "I told you that you should not have done that to him."

It was an hour before he was to clock out. He was shaking, and I could see it. I did not do anything else. He told Dad he had to go home early. He could not control his shaking and had become so ill that he was about to throw up. There was no way a little guy could do anything like that to a grown man.

Dad told him he could finish the shift for him and do his work also. The coworker went home at that very moment. When the next crew came on, they all wondered where he was. He was not here to clock out, and they saw his time card in the outbox. Dad just told them he got sick and had to go home.

I went with Dad many times after that and stayed the night. His coworker never did anything else to me, and I did not do anything else to him. We were at peace with each other once more.

CHAPTER 13

A REVISIT THAT
MUST BE TOLD

DO YOU WANT the child with so much pain to go away? You will have to answer this question for yourself. The title of this book is Hide or Seek. Hiding things of the heart will be replayed every day of your life. Try to understand them—and do not be afraid.

I do not have all the answers to all the questions of the inner working of the brain and heart. I have not accepted everything from those who do to have the right answers for me. I have found peace after years of study. That peace comes from the wisdom of many who gave me the freedom to be myself. I am a seeker, and I have sought the answers that seemed to work best for me. Working with others over the years has helped me help them too—at least I hope so. The little five-year-old is very much still alive and living happily inside me. I do not fear him, and he does not fear me. When looking back over my life, I have discovered that he did not trust anyone. He has just recently begun to trust the adult version of himself. It has taken more than sixty years to do so. I will not break that trust he has given the adult me.

I was told by a very trusted teacher that you cannot go any deeper with someone's pain than you are willing to go with your own. This statement helped me understand why people were not listening to me when I tried to tell my story. They could not relate to the five-year-old and his pain. They may have had their five-year-old memories touched and could not deal with them as a five-year-old. However, listen as deeply as you can, and if it hurts too much, say so. Stop the pain in your life and know there will be somebody who is willing to go to the depth of the abyss with you. It may be yourself. Have a lifeline to tie around your heart when you do. One of the best lifelines I have had is Jesus. When I needed or need Him, He was and is there and here. When I need people, He brought them to me. Not just anyone can help.

It is time to revisit the thoughts of the heart the five-year-old lost. I lost most of the trusted people in my life in the fire. You can find people who seem to take their place, but they are the only ones who can fill that spot. Try placing other people there. Most likely, you will be let down. Let experience rest itself with each person in your life. I am learning to rest on the memories I have of my family. I trust others to be who they are. Hopefully, they know who they are. I have many people in my life, but only a few have proven to be trusted friends. Many will seemingly be your friends until they get what they need from you. You may already know who these people are in your life.

I do not say these things to hurt—only to be truthful with myself. When they need something, I know they will come back again, and I will do my best to help them. This is the life I live. I am mostly all right with it. I have long-distance relationships that are closer than the ones I have close, and these are friends who stayed through the hard times. Bubby would try to make friends with everyone he could, maybe trying to find brothers, but he was disappointed almost every time. These people would come into his life and soon depart, never to be heard from again. He would do his best to stay in touch—but never hear from them again. There was no need to feel sad; he realized it was feeling the pain of loss over and over brought on by the fire.

How deep shall we go? Bubby would like to hear his name again. Not all the time but now and then. He does have another secret; would you like to know it? If you have ever seen the movie Cars, you know there is a rusty, dented tow truck with no hood called Mater. In Cars II, Mater becomes the focus. When they are working on him to make him look better, they try to remove his dents. He says he wants to keep them, but the ones trying to remove his dents do not understand. His said, "If you remove my dents, you remove who I am."

I also have a dent. I know people are not sure how to react to it. I get a lot of stares most of the time from people who meet me for the first time. The longer they stare, the longer I must see what they are like on the inside. Sometimes, I want to walk over and say, "Take a picture—it will last longer." Instead, I try to move on. My dent comes with memories that look at me every time I look in a mirror. My dent represents a family that went through a significant loss. In books like Red Badge of Courage, try to understand the moments in people's lives that stay with them.

I will say a little more about my dent. I worked on removing it because people made me ashamed of it at times—even to the point of secluding myself and never going out in public. I could not do that. I like being around people. They will have to take me as I am or leave me. After some people got to know me, my dent mostly went away. They took the time to see the inside instead of the outside. I try not to say much and let people decide for themselves what they will do. Letting people be themselves is a gift that I do my best to give them. It does not mean I always agree with them. It just means I will not judge them. Bubby still reminds me that others are going through emotions also. Would anybody like to get to know Bubby? Touch my dent—and close your eyes when you do. Be gentle—and do not pull away. When you do, you will be touching Bubby's most inner being and his heart. He is not afraid to let you. Just ask.

Bubby learned to run from things when warranted. He does not run until he has evaluated almost everything that is going on. When you run, you may miss what you need to see the most. Bubby and I watched Dad working at a construction site. They were erecting an elevator that would carry grain to the top of the silo. My cousin was on top, putting the bolts in the belt to hold the small scoops that would carry the grain up, and my dad was standing on the ground turning the pully that rotated the belt. Suddenly, the walls of the elevator began to collapse. Everyone ran for cover.

Dad stepped back and watched it to everyone's amazement. My cousin had no choice but to hang on for dear life. After Dad saw what was happening, he ran. Everyone began to laugh at him for running after the fact.

He said, "Laugh all you want—I was making sure I would not run in the direction of the impending danger."

They all went silent, and then my cousin came climbing down, still shaking a bit. I learned from Dad that day, but I did not realize Bubby had seen him do this very same thing many times before. Running is good, but it is important to know where you are running and why. Most of the time, whatever is chasing you will have to give up.

Bubby had some dreams that I will share. I have remembered my dreams for most of my life. Most were playing and looking forward to the next day. Then there are those dreams that no one wants to dream. It seems you cannot help yourself. They come when you least expect them. These are the dreams that may be trying to tell you that you have unresolved issues in your life.

Are you ready for one? There was a dream where someone was always chasing me. I realized they were trying to kill me. If they could not kill me, they would kill everyone else in the dream, including my family with chainsaws, grenades, guns, knives, ropes, and many other dangerous objects. These were vivid dreams with surround sound that shakes the room. In one dream, the person even attacked the church I was in. The people in the church were destroyed. It seemed there was nothing I could do. Many nights, I would wake up breathless and not wanting to go back to sleep. I was five in most of these dreams—with a grown body. We were fighting together, Bubby and I, and staying to watch what would happen.

The dreams haunted me for years, and I would wake up many nights not ready to go back to sleep. Then I began to fit the puzzle together. I noticed a pattern developing in the many shows I was watching and the things I was learning. Some of the books were painting the same picture. If you are asking what the pattern was, have patience, please. As I remember back to the old cowboy movies, running was not what they did at the OK Corral. Running was not what armies that won did. Sometimes the people would die, but most of the time, they would win. Facing their fears and knowing what they could and would do made them the people who were still standing when everything settled.

I began to work with my dreams instead of running from them. Many nights, I knew I was dreaming. The pleasant dreams were a safe place to try experiments while dreaming. Instead of trying to run in a race, which I cannot do in dreams, I realized I could fly. At first, I would bump the ground as I tried, and then I got to where I could fly higher and higher. At first, fear gripped me because of what would happen if I fell. Overcoming this fear, I would fly a lot. I got to the point of perfect flying, and then I could hold other people's hands and help them fly. In one dream, I held more than ten people, and we were all flying and having so much fun.

I will go back to the danger zone. Dreams that I was not ready to dream again came back fast. I began to put together everything I was learning and brought it into the dreams. I would hide behind objects to see if I could see the murdering person. I could hear them breathing as they shadowed by. Trying my hardest, I never saw their face. I only saw the black robe after they walked by. Why could I not see their face? Was I still too afraid to look—or were they hiding their identity from me?

I did that for a couple of years. One day, I felt Bubby trying to tell me something. I found a quiet place and got really still. I closed my eyes and thought some of the most profound thoughts ever. There was Bubby. I knew who he was and noticed he looked terrified. We did not talk; there was no need. I knew what he was thinking. He was thinking that this person was going to kill him, and I knew that would be the end of me too. Everybody in his family had always protected Bubby, but only one person could save him and keep him alive. We looked long and deep into each other's eyes, and I heard his cry for help and the agony he was in. "Help me please. You are the only one left who can help me and save me."

I told him not to worry that it was all going to end soon, and he would be safe forever after that. He climbed into my arms, and I held him close. He went to sleep and rested. He was trusting me to do what I had to do. A few nights later, the dream came again.

The person was there and was more real than ever and killing everyone and everything around me. The battle went into the sandy field, and we fought. I hit the person, and the person hit me. Over and over, we hit each other. We fought for hours. I could not see who the person was. We had gone all over this field of brown sand, up to one hill and down the next. We found ourselves in an area with quicksand pits. I had gotten the upper hand and was able to knock the person into one of them. The enemy began to sink into the sand fast, and I started to walk away because I had won. I turned to see the person sinking deeper and deeper. The person cried out for mercy and asked me to save them. In a moment of compassion, I did. I had finally recognized the person was a male. I reached my hand out and took him, and his face was covered with the wet sand. I pulled with all the strength I had left, trying to save him now. Knowing that he could still try to kill me, I helped him anyway. I pulled him out to where he was safe, and we lay there totally exhausted. We could hear each other breathing so hard—and no words were spoken during that time.

It was time to face the person I had come to fear my whole life. I would face the enemy who had been trying to kill Bubby. While talking, I asked why he was trying to kill me. He told me he had felt the pain of the little boy and mine for so long that the enemy wanted to help stop it—and the only way he knew was to put Bubby to rest. I cried and was dumbfounded that this was the only way he thought he could help.

We stood and turned to face each other. We reached our hands out, took hold of each other, and pulled ourselves together. I used my handkerchief to clean the enemy's face. The sand was matted from his tears. He was no longer just a person, a blank figure, a mystery, or someone who hated everyone. The sand fell to the ground, and the ground became white stone. As I cleaned, I was shocked at who it was. I could see the pain on his face. I could feel Bubby inside was shocked also. We looked at each other; I knew him and had known him for many years.

I feel I have only lived half my life so far. I tease about the next half of my life to do much more. There are many adventures that I have yet to do. I believe I will go and do so much. I still have so much to learn and experience. My body may be full of pain at times, but it does not stop the joy I have discovered. The joy and hope are much bigger than anything else. I want everyone to know this joy as their own.

CHAPTER 14

THE LAST CHAPTER FOR NOW

THERE IS NEVER a last chapter for the soul. It is the part of us that lives forever. Where we spend that forever is up to us.

It is the last chapter of this book, but it is not the end of the story. The end of the story comes when all is said and done. When I started the book, it was because I felt freedom for the inner child who I had protected my whole life. If we do not protect who we are and what made us the way we are, we will lose what we are supposed to be. If we deny who we are, we deny that we ever existed. We will find ourselves asking over and over, "Who am I?"

To my understanding, we have memories that have been lost—only to be awakened when we see, smell, hear, or touch something that relates to the memory. Some memories we want to forget for various reasons, and others we want to hang onto for life. Maybe something as simple as remembering a loved one who has died. In the days after they die, we think we have lost who they were. The pain of losing someone or something can take away what we want most if we are not careful. Pain is a part of life, and pain tells us something is happening or has happened that needs our attention. It is good to know when we deal with pain, it gets better, or we learn to cope with it. Hiding it or seeking it is a lifelong adventure or a horror story. Which is more important to you? If we close off the pain, our memories may close too. They may hide until something awakes them—maybe at a time that is not the best.

The inner child is happy today because he is alive and well as an adult. Who wants to grow up? The apostle Paul says we are to put away childish things, not to deny them. I know who I am today is who God helped me become. There are days when I am afraid and days when I can take on anything—at least I think I can. Seeking who I am led me to ask God who He saw me as. He has a perfect view of who I am and how I may get where I need to be. I stopped hiding a long time ago. As I was growing up, I learned to protect the inner me from getting hurt over and over by people who wanted to judge me. Many people will do horrible things to the inner you—dare to protect yourself from them.

Sometimes it is not others who are bringing the hurt; it is us. In Star Wars, Luke was going down into the hole to face Darth Vader. When he strikes Darth Vader, Darth Vader's mask comes off—and Luke sees himself. The scene leaves us with questions about what it means. In the end, we see Darth Vader is Luke's father. In reality, the past makes a difference because it affects us today. You are someone who has been wonderfully made for a purpose, and I hope you will fulfill your purpose with energy and delight in God's knowledge and the wisdom of who you are.

If you like what you have read, I want to encourage you to move forward with who you are. Seek what you need to do so you will not be left hiding. If you did not like this book, that is your choice. I respect it. Thank you for buying this book and reading it. Someone once told me that the price of a book is worth it if it is only to glean one thing from it. I have many books that cost too much but became worth the price because each has had something that challenged me or spoke to me.

What freedom we will have when the inner child is not afraid to come out and play. We may even grow into adults who are protected and taught by ourselves. That may be a scary thought, but it is so worth it to grow. Do you wonder why you do things that only a child would do? Think about it for a moment. Maybe you just had one of those a-ha moments. It is your child speaking up or acting out to get your attention. Some people may think what is said here is not valid, but each person must decide for themselves. For way too long, we have allowed others to tell us how to act or think. Now, there are times we need correcting; what child or person does not? We need to weigh the evidence of what is needed for most of us. Children can reteach us things we may have forgotten if we listen carefully. Why a child? The innocence of a pure-hearted child sees things with such a clear vision that God can lead them, which helps us lead others.

Looking at the inner child from an adult perspective will help us protect ourselves—and then we can grow by leaps and bounds. We become the one who has grown and even suffered, at times, through the things we have gone through. Once we are grown—and with God's guidance—we can go back in time to help those parts of our lives that are missing or hidden from ourselves. We may even be able to find those what-ifs of life. We will have a chance to finish the unfinished things we always wanted to finish.

What we fear most is not becoming the person we need to become. There is a time where childlike faith grows to an adult understanding of how Christ cares for the children and blesses them. No longer will we tell the child to go away because Jesus does not have time for them. We will sense and feel His love overcome us and find the peace that our souls look for. Ever feel like screaming? Watch a child and see if they do not scream at times. What is the adult's first response? Stop it? Shut up? What did you tell yourself when you felt like screaming as an adult? Screaming comes, many times, from pain. Sometimes it comes from feeling that we were wronged. I help my child scream when he needs it, but I ask, "Why do you feel the need to scream?" I listen to the answer. It is not always what I think it will be. Sometimes it is something else. It is time for you to answer this one.

Did you catch it? The inner child just stepped out again and spoke? He wants you to know he cares for you and wants the best for you. Maybe someday you can come over and play with him and have fun again. Be not afraid of what is ahead of you—and your past will push you forward into the future. Everything you are today is who you have become from all that has happened to you. Maybe you might ask yourself who you are and ask God who you can be in His grand purpose for your life. Nothing has happened that cannot make things work out in the end if we open our lives up to see what God sees in us.

The ideas, memories, adventures, and dreams have been shared from the memories of a child who missed little while growing up. I often see things differently than others do. It does not make me right and them wrong. We are who we are. You have the freedom to discover so much more in your life if you wish. I wish I could walk with you and see all the marvelous things that shall grow from you seeking you.

When it is time to write the next section of my memories, I will start where I left off here. It does not mean I will not tell more of my birth-to-eight-year-old stories again. They will be ones that were not told in this book. I am already thinking about when I turn nine, which was when my mind and body began to change. "I remember one time ..."

See you in the next book.

CPSIA information can be obtained
at www.ICGtesting.com
Printed in the USA
FSHW010501161220
76937FS